THE BIBLE EXPLORER'S GUIDE

1,000
AMAZING FACTS AND PHOTOS

 ZONDERkidz

ZONDERKIDZ

The Bible Explorer's Guide
Copyright © 2017 by Zondervan

This title is also available as a Zondervan ebook.

Requests for information should be addressed to:

Zonderkidz, 3900 *Sparks Dr. SE, Grand Rapids, Michigan 49546*

ISBN 978-0-310-75810-5

Written by: Nancy I. Sanders
Art direction: Ron Huizinga
Design & layout: Michelle Lenger

Printed in China

17 18 19 20 21 22 /DSC/ 22 21 20 19 18 17 16 15 14 13 12 11 10 9 8 7 6 5 4 3 2 1

THE AMAZING CONTENTS

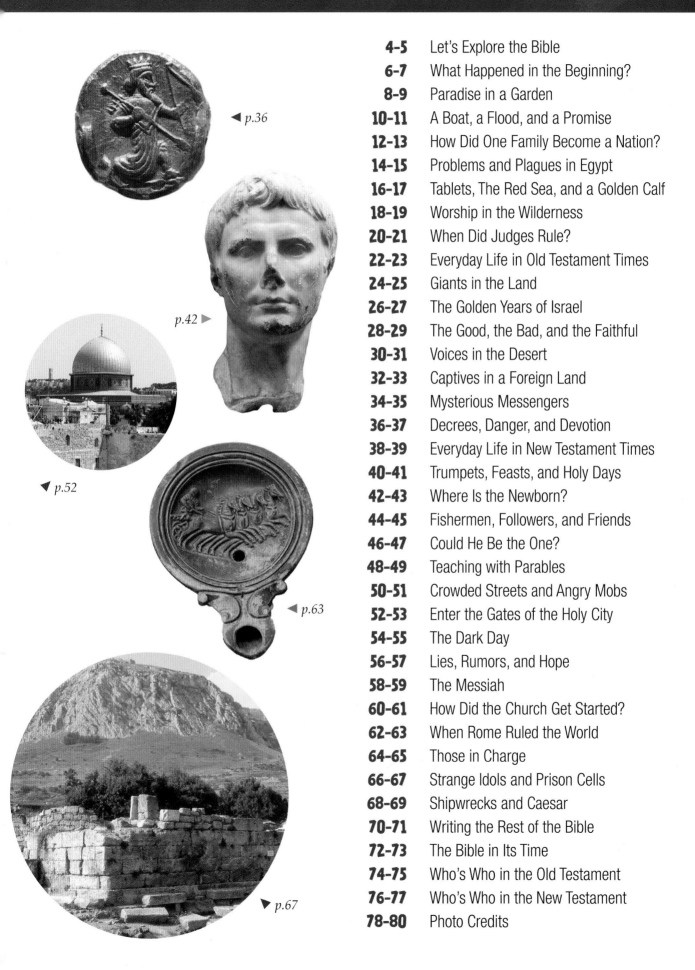

◀ *p.36*

p.42 ▶

◀ *p.52*

◀ *p.63*

▼ *p.67*

4-5	Let's Explore the Bible
6-7	What Happened in the Beginning?
8-9	Paradise in a Garden
10-11	A Boat, a Flood, and a Promise
12-13	How Did One Family Become a Nation?
14-15	Problems and Plagues in Egypt
16-17	Tablets, The Red Sea, and a Golden Calf
18-19	Worship in the Wilderness
20-21	When Did Judges Rule?
22-23	Everyday Life in Old Testament Times
24-25	Giants in the Land
26-27	The Golden Years of Israel
28-29	The Good, the Bad, and the Faithful
30-31	Voices in the Desert
32-33	Captives in a Foreign Land
34-35	Mysterious Messengers
36-37	Decrees, Danger, and Devotion
38-39	Everyday Life in New Testament Times
40-41	Trumpets, Feasts, and Holy Days
42-43	Where Is the Newborn?
44-45	Fishermen, Followers, and Friends
46-47	Could He Be the One?
48-49	Teaching with Parables
50-51	Crowded Streets and Angry Mobs
52-53	Enter the Gates of the Holy City
54-55	The Dark Day
56-57	Lies, Rumors, and Hope
58-59	The Messiah
60-61	How Did the Church Get Started?
62-63	When Rome Ruled the World
64-65	Those in Charge
66-67	Strange Idols and Prison Cells
68-69	Shipwrecks and Caesar
70-71	Writing the Rest of the Bible
72-73	The Bible in Its Time
74-75	Who's Who in the Old Testament
76-77	Who's Who in the New Testament
78-80	Photo Credits

LET'S EXPLORE THE BIBLE

The Bible is the most famous book in the world! More copies have been published and sold than any other book in history. More people have read it, studied it, and talked about it than any other book ever known to exist. But what exactly is the Bible? And who wrote this all-time bestseller? It all started with Moses. He was the first to write things down. But he didn't just write his own words. In Exodus 24:4 we learn that Moses wrote down the very words God said himself. From then on, men were inspired by God to write down God's holy word. They wrote about giants, dangerous plagues, and chariots of fire, mysterious angels, miraculous healings, and raising people from the dead. Most of all, however, they wrote about God's plan. From beginning to end, the Bible talks about God's plan for his people and for you. So get ready for adventure. Let's explore the Bible!

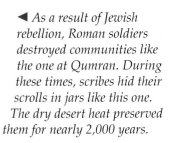

◀ *As a result of Jewish rebellion, Roman soldiers destroyed communities like the one at Qumran. During these times, scribes hid their scrolls in jars like this one. The dry desert heat preserved them for nearly 2,000 years.*

THRILLING DISCOVERY

In 1947 a young Bedouin shepherd lost some of his goats. Looking in a cave, he found several clay jars containing ancient scrolls. Little did he realize he had stumbled onto one of the most important discoveries in the history of the Bible. Over the next 20 years, archaeologists and local people found 28 scrolls. They also discovered 100,000 fragments that pieced together to make 875 more manuscripts. They were 1,000 years older than any other book of the Bible in existence. Many dated back 2,000 years to the time of Jesus. Some were even older than that! Known as the Dead Sea Scrolls, we have learned many things about the history of the Bible from studying them and exploring the region where they were found.

DEVOUT COMMUNITY

This map shows an archaeological site called Qumran. It is in the northwest region of the Dead Sea. It was here that a community of Jews, the Essenes, probably lived. They were there from about 130 BC to AD 68. They copied scrolls of the Hebrew Bible as well as other documents.

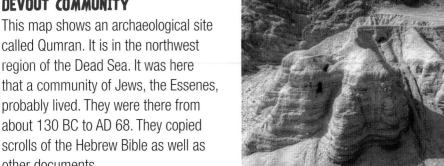

TREASURE HUNTERS

Archaeologists work carefully to dig up treasures from the past. They look for clues to help us understand the Bible, the people who wrote the Bible, and what life was like in Bible times.

▶ *These ancient "pens" were discovered in Qumran. Called a stylus, each is made from a palm leaf. A scribe dipped the pointed end of the stylus into a pot of ink. Then the scribe used the stylus to write.*

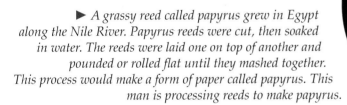

▶ *A grassy reed called papyrus grew in Egypt along the Nile River. Papyrus reeds were cut, then soaked in water. The reeds were laid one on top of another and pounded or rolled flat until they mashed together. This process would make a form of paper called papyrus. This man is processing reeds to make papyrus.*

Did You Know?

The most famous scroll found at Qumran is the Isaiah scroll. Twenty-four feet long, it is written on 17 sheets of leather sewn together end to end. This scroll contains the entire text of the book of Isaiah. Comparing the words on the Dead Sea Scrolls to the Bible we have today shows us how accurate the process has been over thousands of years to preserve God's Word from each generation to the next.

▲ *The different manuscripts found in Qumran were written in Hebrew, Aramaic, Arabic, Latin, and Greek.*

WHAT HAPPENED IN THE BEGINNING?

The Bible says that in the beginning God created the whole world in six days. God had the power and wisdom to create a world exactly how he wanted and in a way he knew was best. Some people debate whether God created the world in seven actual days or if each "day" lasted longer than 24 hours. But the truth is all that matters—that God created the world and humans in his image.

HEBREW CALENDAR

In the year 2000, the date was 5761 on the Hebrew calendar. According to Jewish tradition, the Hebrew calendar starts with the year the world was created.

▶ This ancient Hebrew mosaic shows the zodiac inside the circle and the seasons of the year in each corner.

◀ Ibises have long, down-curved bills, and usually feed as a group, probing mud for food items, usually crustaceans.

QUESTIONS AND ANSWERS

In the book of Job, God asks Job important questions such as, "Who gives the ibis wisdom or gives the rooster understanding?" (Job 38:36). The answer is God. God also asks Job, "Does the hawk take flight by your wisdom and spread its wings toward the south?" (Job 39:26). The answer is God. In his great wisdom, God designed animals with instincts to know when and where to migrate, what to eat, or how to build a nest.

DAY ONE:
God made light.

DAY TWO:
God made sky and water.

DAY THREE:
God made seas and land and plants.

SIR ISAAC NEWTON

Isaac Newton (1642–1726) is one of the most famous scientists who ever lived. He read and studied his Bible daily. He said that the more he investigated the amazing details of creation as a scientist, the better he knew God.

A MARVELOUS DESIGNER

What if you saw a sandcastle? Would you think the waves created it by chance? Of course not! You would know someone built it. It's the same with creation. The more scientists study it, the more we understand it couldn't have happened by chance. Someone with intelligence designed the marvels of the universe and put everything in its place. The Bible tells us that this someone is God.

Did You Know?

Jesus is God. And God created the world and everything in it. Colossians 1:15–16 says, "The Son is the image of the invisible God, the firstborn over all creation. For in him all things were created: things in heaven and on earth, visible and invisible, whether thrones or powers or rulers or authorities; all things have been created through him and for him." To learn more about creation, read Genesis 1:1–2:3.

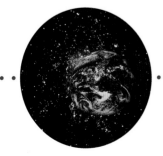

DAY FOUR:
God made the sun and moon and stars.

DAY FIVE:
God made fish and birds.

DAY SIX:
God made land animals and man and woman.

DAY SEVEN:
God rested and enjoyed his creation.

PARADISE IN A GARDEN

Who were the first man and woman? How did they get here? What part of the world did they come from? People have wondered about these questions for thousands of years. Some archaeologists have devoted their lives to searching for clues. Many scholars have debated for years about how to interpret the meaning of scientific data and material culture from ancient times. Every person seems to have an opinion. Today, with modern technology as well as the Bible itself, we know more than any other generation.

RED EARTH

Genesis 2:7 says God formed the first man from dust. The name Adam sounds like the Hebrew word for "red." In the mountains of Turkey, the dirt is very red. This causes some scholars to speculate that the lost rivers of Eden ran through this region.

▼ *At 1,780 miles long, the Euphrates River is the longest river in this part of the world. Beginning in the country of Turkey, it flows through Syria and then joins the Tigris River before running into the Persian Gulf.*

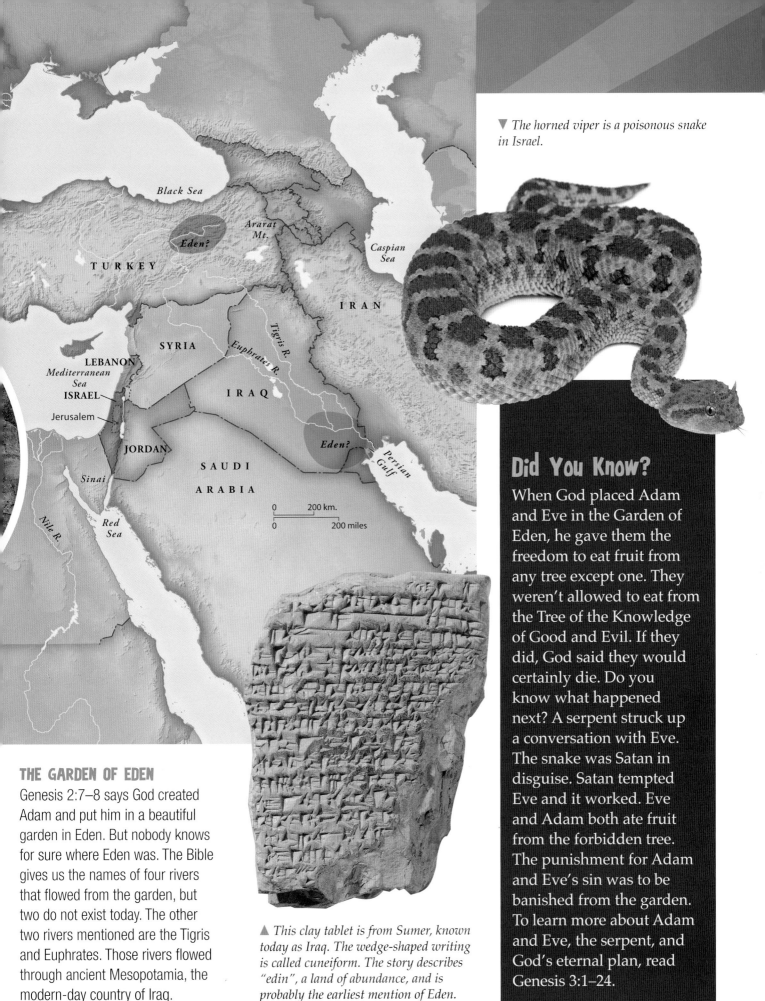

Black Sea

Ararat Mt.

Eden?

Caspian Sea

TURKEY

IRAN

SYRIA

Euphrates R.

Tigris R.

LEBANON
Mediterranean Sea
ISRAEL

Jerusalem

IRAQ

Eden?

Persian Gulf

JORDAN

SAUDI ARABIA

Sinai

Nile R.

Red Sea

0   200 km.

0   200 miles

THE GARDEN OF EDEN

Genesis 2:7–8 says God created Adam and put him in a beautiful garden in Eden. But nobody knows for sure where Eden was. The Bible gives us the names of four rivers that flowed from the garden, but two do not exist today. The other two rivers mentioned are the Tigris and Euphrates. Those rivers flowed through ancient Mesopotamia, the modern-day country of Iraq.

▲ *This clay tablet is from Sumer, known today as Iraq. The wedge-shaped writing is called cuneiform. The story describes "edin", a land of abundance, and is probably the earliest mention of Eden.*

Did You Know?

When God placed Adam and Eve in the Garden of Eden, he gave them the freedom to eat fruit from any tree except one. They weren't allowed to eat from the Tree of the Knowledge of Good and Evil. If they did, God said they would certainly die. Do you know what happened next? A serpent struck up a conversation with Eve. The snake was Satan in disguise. Satan tempted Eve and it worked. Eve and Adam both ate fruit from the forbidden tree. The punishment for Adam and Eve's sin was to be banished from the garden. To learn more about Adam and Eve, the serpent, and God's eternal plan, read Genesis 3:1–24.

9

A BOAT, A FLOOD, AND A PROMISE

There are over 200 accounts of a huge flood in the writings of ancient cultures. The story in the Bible describes how Noah's sons and their wives spread out around the world after the floodwaters dried up. The flood story was likely retold by various storytellers in different cultures who added details from their own traditions.

FLOOD STORIES

China, Hawaii, Mexico, Ireland, and Greece are just a few of the places that have stories about a flood. For example, the Epic of Gilgamesh comes from ancient Nineveh in the kingdom of Babylonia. It tells of a king learning about the flood by traveling through the "underworld."

◀ *Noah took pairs of every kind of animal into the ark.*

Did you Know?

The book of Genesis says pairs of every kind of animal came to Noah. But he also brought in seven pairs of some animals that were good for food. After the flood, the animals were released to multiply and fill up the earth again. To learn more about Noah, the animals, the ark, and the flood, read Genesis 6:9–9:17.

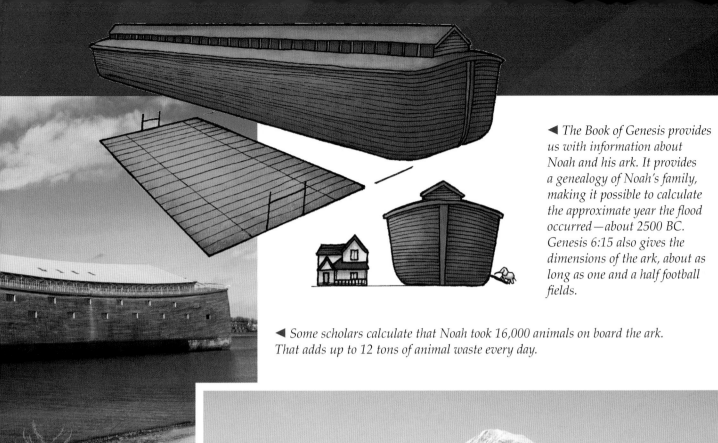

◄ *The Book of Genesis provides us with information about Noah and his ark. It provides a genealogy of Noah's family, making it possible to calculate the approximate year the flood occurred—about 2500 BC. Genesis 6:15 also gives the dimensions of the ark, about as long as one and a half football fields.*

◄ *Some scholars calculate that Noah took 16,000 animals on board the ark. That adds up to 12 tons of animal waste every day.*

► *As the waters of the flood dried up, the ark settled on the mountains of Ararat. Even though many explorers have looked for the remains of the ark, it has never been found.*

A SPECIAL PROMISE

The Bible says God sent a flood to wash away sinful people from the world. But the rainbow God sends is a sign of God's promise never to send a worldwide flood again. Whenever you see a rainbow, remember this special promise of God.

WORLD'S FIRST SKYSCRAPER

Noah's descendants spread eastward. They found a flat region and settled there. Then they had an idea. They'd build a tower so high it would reach up to heaven. The Bible says they were trying to make a name for themselves. Instead, God confused their language so they couldn't finish the Tower of Babel. From there, they spread out all over the world, speaking in many different languages.

HOW DID ONE FAMILY BECOME A NATION?

The ancient city of Ur was a center of business, wealth, and culture. Abram, his wife Sarai, and the rest of their family called Ur home. In the book of Genesis, God called Abram to leave his home and move. God promised to give this new land of Harran to Abram and his descendants forever. Did Abram complain or refuse to budge? No, Abraham took his wife, all their possessions, and a nephew named Lot, and followed God's lead. He stepped out in faith. He chose to believe God and the promises God made to him.

◀ *This ancient game was discovered in a tomb in Ur.*

PITCHING THEIR TENTS

Traveling in Abraham's day was not the same as today. It was dangerous. There were wild animals, robbers, and warring kings. Plus the wilderness was hot, dusty, and dry. Abraham and his family lived in tents as they traveled.

◀ *Cloth for tents was usually woven from goat's hair.*

CENTER OF TRADE

Abram was born in the city of Ur in 2166 BC, at the height of its wealth and strength. The power of its kings stretched westward from Ur to the Mediterranean Sea. Ur was joined to the Euphrates River by canals, establishing it as a center of trade within the ancient world.

▶ *Most houses in Ur were built from bricks of baked mud. Rooms were often designed to surround a central courtyard.*

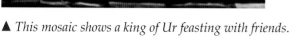
▲ *This mosaic shows a king of Ur feasting with friends.*

Abraham and the Twelve Tribes of Israel

ABRAHAM'S FAMILY TREE

The Bible gives us the historical account of Abraham and how his family became a nation. It tells about Abraham's son Ishmael, Abraham's son of promise Isaac, and his grandson Jacob (who eventually became known as Israel). His 12 great-grandsons became the 12 tribes of the nation of Israel.

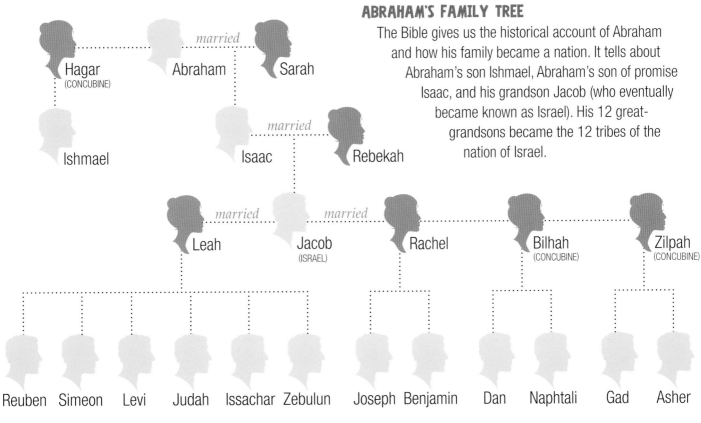

Hagar (CONCUBINE) — *married* — Abraham : Sarah

Ishmael

Isaac — *married* — Rebekah

Leah — *married* — Jacob (ISRAEL) — *married* — Rachel   Bilhah (CONCUBINE)   Zilpah (CONCUBINE)

Reuben   Simeon   Levi   Judah   Issachar   Zebulun   Joseph   Benjamin   Dan   Naphtali   Gad   Asher

THE COMMAND TO MOVE

When Abram and his family first left Ur, they settled in Harran. Abram was 75 years old when he heard God call him to leave Harran and move 450 miles southwest to the land of the Canaanites. At the time of the covenant, God changed Abram and Sarai's names to Abraham and Sarah.

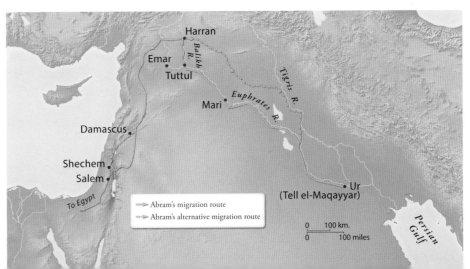

Harran

Emar
Tuttul
Balikh R.

Mari
Euphrates R.

Tigris R.

Damascus

Shechem
Salem

To Egypt

Ur (Tell el-Maqayyar)

→ Abram's migration route
→ Abram's alternative migration route

0   100 km.
0   100 miles

Persian Gulf

The history of Israel includes a lot of time spent in Egypt. It is one family's story set against the backdrop of ancient Egypt. How did this happen? Sometime during the 19th century BC, a young man named Joseph was one of 12 brothers. Joseph was Jacob's favorite son. His brothers were jealous, so they sold him into Egypt as a slave. There, Joseph became the second in command over Egypt. A severe famine hit the land. Everyone was starving, so all 11 brothers and their families moved to Egypt where they were reunited with Joseph and given food.

▲ *This scene was painted on the walls of a wealthy man's tomb at Beni Hasan. Hieroglyphic writing above the painting says these visitors are going to Egypt. The people are from a region similar to where Joseph lived before he became a slave in Egypt.*

LOCUST SWARMS

On November 17, 2004, swarms of pink locusts darkened the skies above the Giza pyramids near Cairo. Frightened people ran away and hid. One of the ten plagues God sent to Egypt through Moses was a swarm of locusts worse than this.

MEASURING GRAIN

Pharaoh, the ruler of Egypt, had a dream, and no one could tell him what it meant. Joseph was able to explain that God was warning Pharaoh that the land would suffer from a great famine. He gave Joseph the important job of gathering enough grain during years of plenty to feed the entire nation during years of famine.

► *This painting was found in the Tomb of Menna from around 1400 BC. It shows officials measuring grain for tax, much as Joseph did to store grain in Egypt to prepare for the famine.*

SLAVE LABOR

The Israelite slaves were forced to mix mud from the Nile River with straw left over from grain in the field. This mixture was shaped into bricks and baked under the brutal sun of Egypt. Endless supplies of bricks were needed to build Pharaoh's colossal monuments and towering temples.

► *Mud bricks dried in the sun are still used today in parts of Africa and Asia.*

▲ *Giant statues of Ramses and his queen.*

UNSOLVED MYSTERY

Archaeologists and Bible scholars have tried for years to unlock a mystery. Which hard-hearted pharaoh ruled in Egypt when Moses arrived? Even though archaeological evidence isn't 100% sure, many scholars think it was Ramses II.

THE FIRST PASSOVER

Four hundred years after Joseph's family moved to Egypt, they still lived there—as slaves. So God sent them a deliverer—Moses. There was just one problem. Pharaoh refused to let the Israelites go. So God sent ten plagues against the Egyptians. The tenth and final plague was the death of the firstborn sons.

Moses warned Pharaoh that the Lord would go through the land at midnight and kill the firstborn sons in all of Egypt. However, the families of Israel were instructed to sacrifice a lamb and spread its blood on the sides and tops of their doorways. The Lord would pass over every house where he saw the blood. Their sons were safe. Not until his own son was killed that night did Pharaoh give permission for the Israelites to leave Egypt.

Did You Know?

Joseph forgave his brothers. Genesis 50:20 says Joseph told his brothers, "You intended to harm me, but God intended it for good to accomplish what is now being done, the saving of many lives." Joseph invited his brothers and their families to move to Egypt and stay in the land of Goshen (shown here).

The Israelites fled from Egypt and the pharaoh. But soon they realized they were blocked in by the Red Sea. The Israelites panicked. But God parted the waters, and the Israelites marched across on dry ground. Once they were safely on the other side, they turned around and looked. Pharaoh and his chariots were close behind. But the waters of the Red Sea crashed down over them and swept them away. Rejoicing, Moses and the Israelites turned their backs on Egypt. They spent the next 40 years in the wilderness on their way toward Canaan, the land God had promised to them. This incredible journey is known as the Exodus. It probably took place around 1446 BC.

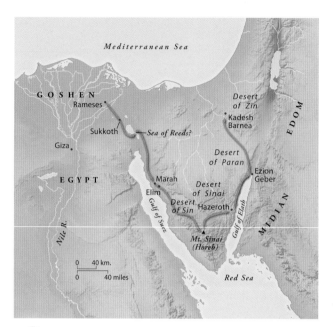

THE NEXT GENERATION

The Israelites wandered in the wilderness for 40 years. Most of the original slaves released from Egypt were dead and were replaced by their children, a new generation of fearless warriors.

◄ *This is a possible route from Egypt to the Promised Land.*

▼ *When the Israelites left Egypt, they did not go empty-handed. The Egyptians gave them gifts of expensive silver and gold jewelry along with other riches.*

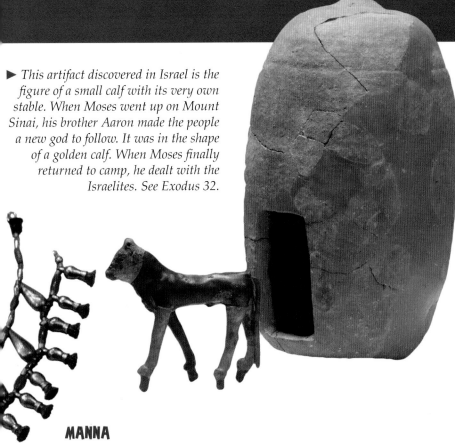

▶ *This artifact discovered in Israel is the figure of a small calf with its very own stable. When Moses went up on Mount Sinai, his brother Aaron made the people a new god to follow. It was in the shape of a golden calf. When Moses finally returned to camp, he dealt with the Israelites. See Exodus 32.*

MANNA

God provided the Israelites with bread and meat as they wandered in the desert. He sent quail and manna. "Manna" means "What is it?" in Hebrew. It was a special bread from heaven. It rained down each night and covered the ground like dew. After it dried, it looked like thin flakes of frost. The Israelites boiled or baked it into small cakes. It tasted sweet, like pastries made with olive oil. God provided manna for 40 years until the Israelites left the desert and entered the Promised Land where they could find plenty of food.

◀ *Their march stopped short when the Israelites came to the banks of the mighty Red Sea. How could that many people and animals ever cross its deep waters? To make matters worse, Pharaoh galloped after them in his chariot. All the chariots, horsemen, and soldiers of Egypt raced behind him.*

Did you Know?

The Israelites set up camp in the Desert of Sinai at the foot of Mount Sinai. Moses then hiked to the top to meet with God. Two stone tablets were given to Moses. On them were written the Ten Commandments. These rules for right-living are a part of the covenant God made with the Israelites.

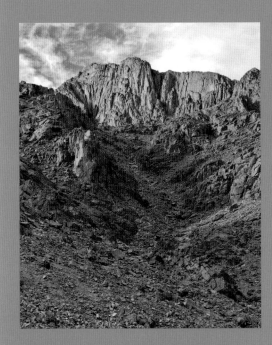

▲ *The Bible mentions this oasis at Marah where God performed a miracle, giving the Israelites water.*

WORSHIP IN THE WILDERNESS

The Israelites hadn't been away from Egypt very long when God assigned them an important job. They were chosen to build a holy place for worship. The Israelites worked steadily for nearly a year while camped at the foot of Mount Sinai. Finally, the Tent of Meeting was finished. A cloud settled down over the tabernacle, and the glory of the Lord filled the tent.

GIVING TO GOD

Everyone was invited to bring supplies for the building project. The people brought so much gold, silver, and bronze they couldn't use it all. Then all the skilled workers such as engravers, designers, perfumers, embroiderers, and weavers got busy.

The Tent of Meeting stood inside curtains held up by gold covered wooden posts. The tent itself was divided into two rooms. The first room was called the Holy Place. It held important pieces of furniture. Fragrant smoke rose every morning and evening from the altar of incense. A holy bread offering from each of the 12 tribes was kept on the table of shewbread. Light from the seven-branched lampstand filled the room. Behind a curtain was the second room known as the Most Holy Place. This was where the Ark of the Covenant was kept. Only once a year and only the high priest could enter this very sacred room.

▶ *Wood from the acacia tree was used to build the tabernacle, the Ark of the Covenant, and the other furniture used in the Tent of Meeting.*

▲ *Each time the Israelites moved their camp, the Levites carried the tabernacle and its furniture. The Levites were one of the 12 tribes of Israel. Aaron's descendants were appointed as priests. The rest of the Levites were given specific duties to help care for the tabernacle.*

◀ *Special oils were used to anoint the priests who served in the tabernacle. These oils could be stored in a jar such as this alabaster one.*

▶ *Aaron, the brother of Moses, was appointed first high priest. His clothing was very unique, and each piece held important meaning. Over his chest he wore a breastplate of 12 precious stones. Each stone represented one of the 12 tribes of Israel. His shorter blue robe was called an ephod. Around its hem hung decorations of pomegranates and golden bells.*

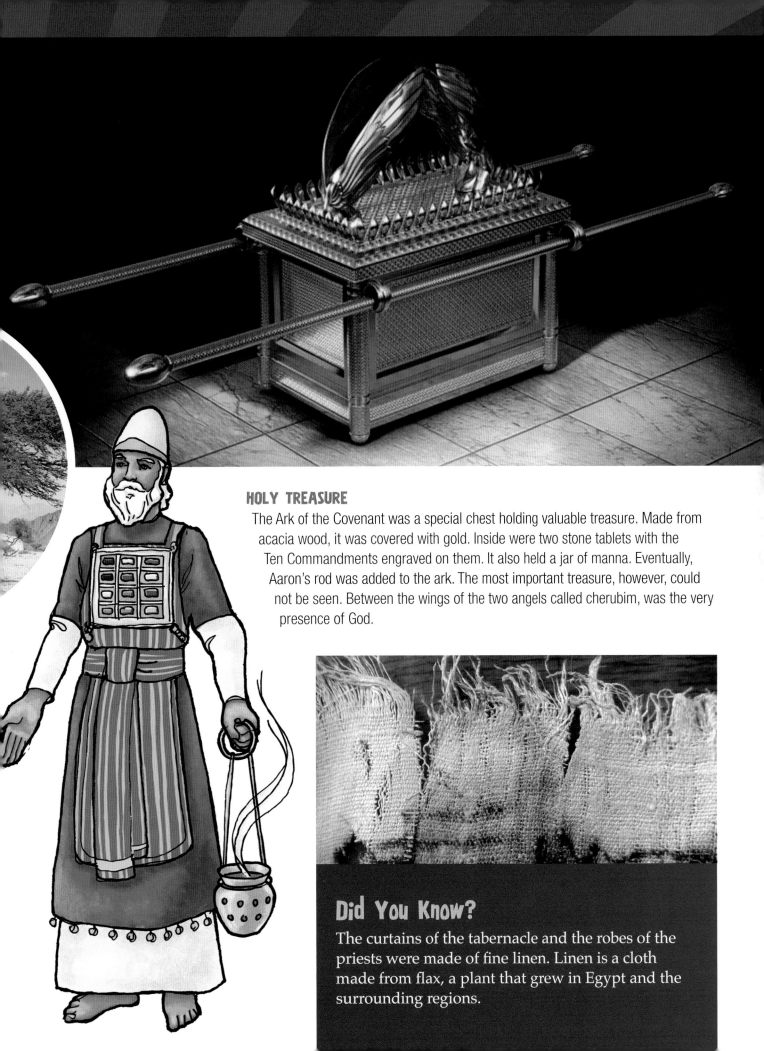

HOLY TREASURE

The Ark of the Covenant was a special chest holding valuable treasure. Made from acacia wood, it was covered with gold. Inside were two stone tablets with the Ten Commandments engraved on them. It also held a jar of manna. Eventually, Aaron's rod was added to the ark. The most important treasure, however, could not be seen. Between the wings of the two angels called cherubim, was the very presence of God.

Did You Know?

The curtains of the tabernacle and the robes of the priests were made of fine linen. Linen is a cloth made from flax, a plant that grew in Egypt and the surrounding regions.

WHEN DID JUDGES RULE?

From about 1406–1050 BC, the Israelites lived in the Promised Land. Their leaders, such as Joshua and Moses, had died. Some Hebrews remained faithful to God and his laws, but many did not. So many people did whatever seemed right in their own opinion. Six major judges ruled during these centuries, mostly as military leaders. Unfortunately, many of these leaders were no more faithful to God than the people.

AMAZING ARTIFACTS

Ekron, a powerful city in Philistia, flourished in the days of the judges. Beginning in 1981, archaeologists excavated this site known as Tel Miqne. One of the most exciting finds was a stone with writing carved into it. It listed five Philistine rulers and identified the name of the city as Ekron.

INHERITING THE LAND

After Joshua and his armies conquered the new land, it was divided among the 12 tribes of Israel. This included the two half-tribes of Joseph—Ephraim and Manasseh. The tribe of Levi did not receive its own large portion of land. Instead, they were given specific towns to live in among the other tribes.

▶ *Loom for weaving cloth.*

DECEITFUL TRAP

Delilah is one of the most well-known Philistines in the Bible. Her story intertwines with Samson, one of Israel's judges. In love with Delilah, Samson was caught in a trap when the Philistines recruited her to spy on him. As part of her trickery to discover the source of his strength, Delilah wove Samson's long hair into a loom. It wasn't until she cut Samson's hair, however, that the Philistines were able to capture their hated opponent and make him a slave.

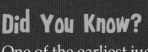

▶ Many iron artifacts such as this knife have been discovered at Ekron.

◀ Kitchen in the Western Palace at Ebla, 4,000–3,000 BC. Samson would have likely used a saddle quern such as these to grind grain as a slave.

▲ This Philistine soldier wears the typical feathered headdress of his uniform.

Did You Know?

One of the earliest judges was a woman named Deborah. People came to her in the hill country of Ephraim to settle their arguments. She also helped lead their armies in a victorious battle. To learn more about Deborah, read Judges 4:1–5:31.

▶ Deborah held court under a palm tree called the Palm of Deborah.

FIERCE ENEMIES

The Philistines were one of Israel's fiercest enemies. They were the only culture in the region that knew the technology for making weapons from iron. Iron was a much stronger metal than bronze that was used by the Hebrews and other Canaanites.

EVERYDAY LIFE IN OLD TESTAMENT TIMES

The period of the judges lasted over 400 years. It was during this era that Ruth, a widow from Moab, traveled to Bethlehem with her mother-in-law, Naomi. Ruth eventually married a man named Boaz. Ruth and Boaz had a son named Obed. His son was Jesse, and Jesse's son was David. The era of the judges eventually came to an end during David's lifetime. As Israel's last judge, Samuel anointed the first king of Israel, King Saul. When King Saul failed to lead the nation according to God's guidance, Samuel anointed a young shepherd named David. Samuel announced that David would be Israel's next king. This David was Boaz and Ruth's great-grandson.

OLIVE PRESS

Olive trees grew in abundance in Israel. Olive presses such as this were used to press down on the olives and squeeze out the oil. This oil was prized for its many uses including cooking and eating, medicine, and as an insect repellent.

◀ *Stones or heavy weights were strapped to the beam of the olive press to help squeeze out the oil.*

TYPICAL HOME

The typical house in Israel during Bible times had four rooms. The main room at the center of the house was an open courtyard without a roof. This large room was flanked by two more rooms. One long room was at the back. Many families kept their donkey, goat, or cow in the courtyard or a side room. This kept their livestock safe from lions, bears, or thieves. Olive oil, barley, and water were stored in the house in large pots, baskets, or animal skins. Often, stairs in the house led up to a flat roof where people would sleep during the hot summer months. The roof was also used for a variety of purposes such as drying flax.

▲ *This shows a model of a four-room house in Israel.*

WINNOWING GRAIN

Part of the harvest work involved winnowing the grain. When it was windy, wheat or barley seeds were tossed up into the air with a special tool called a winnowing fork. The wind blew away the chaff, the dry husk that covered the seeds. The heavier grain fell to the ground. The grain was then collected and stored in baskets or pottery jars until it was ready to be cooked or made into bread.

◀ *This stone pit, built around 790 BC, was a place for storing grain.*

AGRICULTURAL COMMUNITIES

During these years, most families earned their living as farmers. Many kept goats, sheep, cattle, and donkeys. Wheat, barley, and flax were planted in the fields surrounding the towns and villages. Olive trees produced oil and there were vineyards of grapes.

▼ *A shepherd and his flock of sheep.*

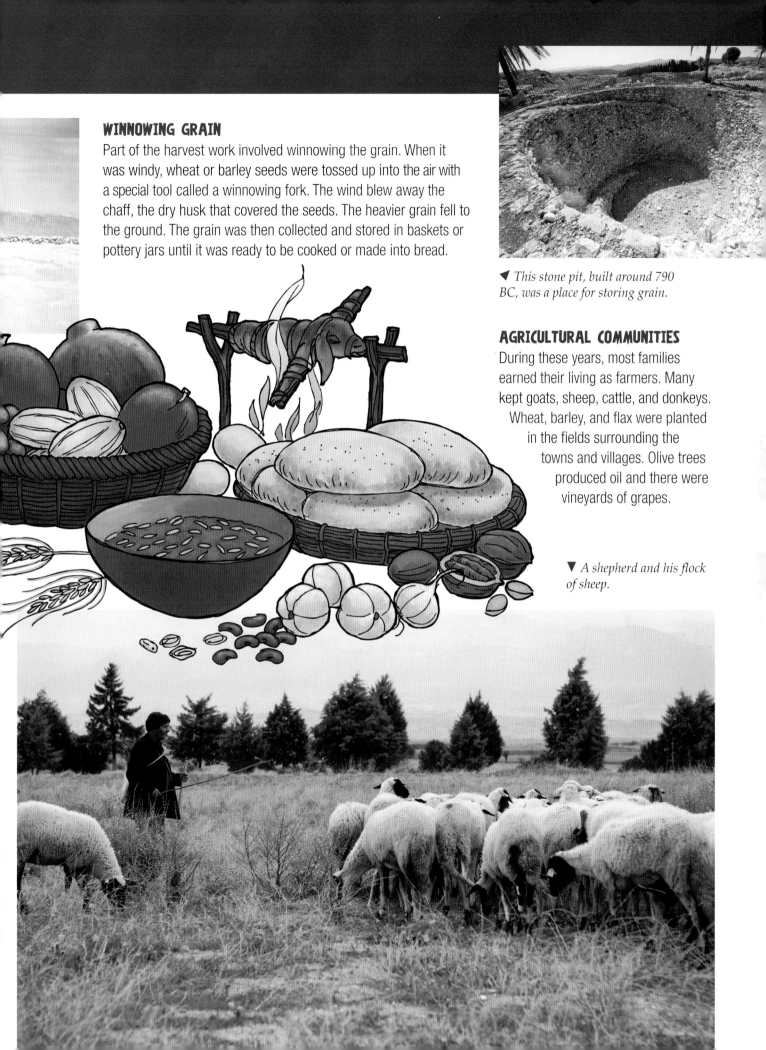

GIANTS IN THE LAND

The Bible centers much of its content on King David and his descendants. Yet nothing in history outside of the Bible had ever been found about King David. Similarly, the Hittites are mentioned in the Bible 47 times yet are not mentioned in any other historical source. This caused some Bible critics to declare neither existed. All this changed in the last century however. Artifacts have been found that prove the existence of both King David and the Hittites.

SHEPHERD BOY

Born in the village of Bethlehem, David was the great-grandson of Ruth and Boaz. The youngest of eight sons, David watched his father's sheep. David also played the harp and wrote many songs while shepherding. The words from some of those songs became part of the Psalms, one of the books in the Old Testament of the Bible.

► *This ninth century BC tablet was discovered in 1993 in northern Israel at Tel Dan. It mentions Ahaziah of the "house of David." The phrase "house of David" refers to the kings who ruled as David's descendants.*

Map labels:
HAMATH
Mediterranean Sea
PHOENICIA
Lebo Hamath
Syrian Desert
Sea of Galilee
Jordan R.
PHILISTIA
Jerusalem
Dead Sea
Eastern Desert
Sinai Desert
Ezion Geber

David's Expansion
Saul's Kingdom
0 10 km.
0 10 miles

UNITED KINGDOM

When King Saul and several of his sons died in a battle against the Philistines, David was anointed king over his own tribe of Judah. The last of Saul's sons ruled the rest of Israel. After seven and a half years, Saul's son was assassinated. Then the people of that kingdom asked David to be their king too. David was anointed king over all of Israel. He ruled for 33 years.

Did You Know?

The Gihon Spring provided fresh water to the city of Jerusalem. The Jebusites who owned the city built a tunnel to the spring. In a daring exploit, David's men climbed up the water shaft and took the stronghold by surprise. David built a royal palace there. Jerusalem was established as the political and religious capital of Israel.

▼ These weapons are some of the earliest ever found in Israel.

THE IRON AGE

At first, only the Hittites knew how to make weapons from iron. When David fought Goliath, only King Saul and his son Jonathan had swords and spears. The other Hebrew soldiers used sticks, farm tools, or rocks and slings as weapons. After David became king, he conquered the Philistines as well as the southern region of Edom. Rich deposits of iron and copper were mined in the dry desert wasteland. This was a turning point in the history of Israel. With the possession of Edom, King David brought the Iron Age to Israel. He now had enough iron to make all the strong weapons and tools they needed. Under King David's reign, Israel became one of the strongest nations in the land.

FACING THE GIANT

The Philistine Goliath stood over nine feet tall. He wore a coat of bronze armor that weighed 125 pounds. The iron point on his spear weighed 15 pounds. This giant challenged the army of Israel to fight. David was the only one brave enough to step forward. The shepherd boy whirled his sling and hurled one stone at the giant. It hit him in the forehead. Goliath crashed to the ground.

▶ Round rocks were often used as sling stones. To throw them, a stone was fitted into a leather pouch with leather straps tied to its ends. As a shepherd, David hurled stones with deadly accuracy to hit lions or bears that attacked his father's sheep.

25

After King David's death, his son Solomon became king of Israel. The years King Solomon ruled (about 970–930 BC) were the most glorious in the history of Israel. It was an era of peace, power, and riches. In 2 Chronicles 1:15 it says "the king made silver and gold as common in Jerusalem as stones." In addition, King Solomon also made his mark in history for his great wisdom and his writings. Many of the Proverbs in the Old Testament were written by King Solomon. The crowning achievement of King Solomon, however, was the construction of the magnificent temple in Jerusalem.

▶ *This is a model of the lampstand that burned olive oil in the temple. King Solomon placed ten lampstands in front of the Most Holy Place.*

GOLDEN TREASURE

The temple in Jerusalem took seven years to build. The top of Mount Moriah was chosen as the holy site. King Solomon used a vast workforce including 80,000 stonecutters who labored in the mountains to quarry large, expensive stones for its foundation. Then he built the temple with boards of cedar and juniper and covered it with pure gold and precious stones. Inside and out, the temple shimmered with gold. Even the nails were made of gold! Elaborate carvings of palm trees, pomegranates, and winged angels called cherubim decorated the walls.

CEDAR OF LEBANON

Wood was needed to build the temple. King Hiram of Tyre agreed to send logs to King Solomon cut from the tall, majestic cedars of Lebanon. Solomon sent 30,000 men to Lebanon to help with the enormous task.

FORTIFIED CITIES

A vital trade route ran through Solomon's kingdom from Egypt north to Damascus. Solomon strengthened three major cities along this road—Gezer, Megiddo, and Hazor. Archaeologists have uncovered many artifacts in these cities dating from the days of King Solomon.

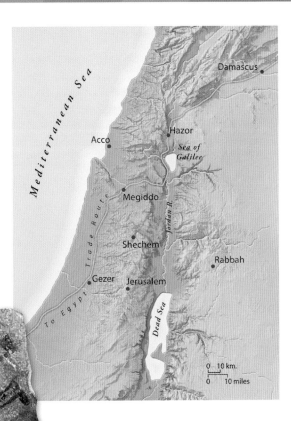

▼ *King Solomon built himself a royal throne from ivory. It was overlaid with pure gold. King Solomon's throne may have looked like this.*

TEMPLE RECEIPT

Broken pieces of pottery were used for many purposes, including writing receipts. This is a receipt from 800 BC. It was given for a donation of three silver shekels to the temple. This is the earliest writing ever found outside of the Bible that mentions the temple.

▼ *Hebrew writing reads from right to left.*

Did You Know?

A huge celebration took place the day King Solomon brought the ark of the covenant into the temple. Nearly everyone in Israel gathered for the special event. The priests put the ark inside the Most Holy Place. Then the priests joined the crowds outside to worship with instruments and singing. To learn more about this special day, read 2 Chronicles 5:1–14.

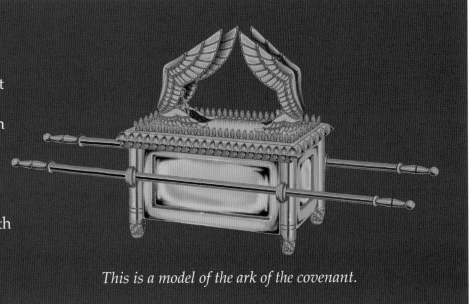

This is a model of the ark of the covenant.

THE GOOD, THE BAD, AND THE FAITHFUL

Artifacts from Bible times bring the events and people of that time to life while also verifying the historic accuracy of the Bible. People are able to study the lifestyle of men and women of the time as well as learn about the rulers—both good and bad. And if you read the Bible, you know that there were some really bad people in authority back then. So God finally lifted his hand of protection. Powerful Assyrian armies swept over the land. Israel fell first in 722 BC. With the rise of mighty Babylon, destruction came to Judah when Jerusalem fell in 586 BC.

ISRAEL'S NEW KING

Jeroboam I established his own political capital in Shechem. He also built Israel's own place to worship so his people would not have to travel to the temple in Jerusalem. He set up two golden calves to worship instead of God. One was in Bethel and one was in the city of Dan.

▶ *Excavations at the city of Dan show the reconstructed platform where the king of Israel sat on his throne at the city gate.*

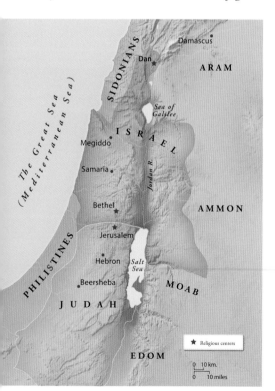

DIVIDED KINGDOMS

After King Solomon died, his son Rehoboam reigned (about 930–913 BC). He continued the line of kings in Judah. But the other tribes (except Benjamin) did not like how harsh the young king ruled. They broke away and crowned their own king. Rehoboam ruled over Judah in the south and Jeroboam I ruled over Israel in the north.

KING OMRI

Omri became the sixth king in Israel. He was more evil than all the kings before him. He also moved the capital of Israel to the city of Samaria. Archaeologists have discovered the ruins of Omri's palace in Samaria.

MOABITE STONE

The kingdom of Israel fought back and forth with Moab, their neighbor to the east. This ancient stone records some of this conflict. The writing says in part, "I, Mesha, king of Moab, made this monument to commemorate deliverance from Israel. My father reigned over Moab thirty years, and I reigned after my father. Omri, king of Israel, oppressed Moab many days and his son after him. But I warred against the king of Israel, and drove him out, and took his cities."

▲ *This stone can be seen at the Louvre in Paris, France.*

◄ *Shalmaneser III (859–824 BC) was a powerful king of Assyria.*

◄ *Gigantic stone bulls with wings and human heads guarded the palace of Sargon II (722–705 BC). A fierce Assyrian general, Sargon became king when Shalmaneser died. Sargon continued a two-year siege on Israel's capital of Samaria until it fell.*

◄ *Discovered in 1846, this impressive four-sided monument stands six and a half feet tall. One scene from the Black Obelisk shows the Israelites bringing tribute similar to how people pay taxes today. Writing on the Black Obelisk reads, "Jehu, son of Omri."*

BLACK OBELISK

One of the most remarkable archaeological finds from Bible history was this tall black stone. The carvings show the Israelites and King Jehu (or his representative) honoring King Shalmaneser III of Assyria. The text, written in cuneiform, tells of King Jehu bringing tribute. He brought "gold, a golden bowl, a golden beaker, golden goblets, golden pitchers, lead, a royal staff, a javelin."

Did you Know?

The book of the law was lost. During the reign of Josiah, king of Judah (640–609 BC) the priests found the holy scroll. When they read it to King Josiah, he tore his robes in dismay. They had not been following God or his holy ways. In a great ceremony, King Josiah read the book aloud to the people and rededicated the nation back to God. To learn more about King Josiah, read 2 Chronicles 34:1–33.

Found among the Dead Sea Scrolls, this fragment with Deuteronomy 5:1-6:1 dates to the first century BC and is one of the earliest artifacts containing the Ten Commandments.

Prophets were holy men and women who shared God's messages with people. One of the earliest prophets was Samuel, the "king's prophet." God chose Samuel to anoint the first two kings of Israel, Saul and David. During each king's reign after that, the voices of the prophets continued to be heard. Some prophets, like Isaiah, ministered for decades and to different kings. Other self-proclaimed prophets didn't even listen to God but pronounced their own message. Some prophets had one or two short prophecies. Many wrote down God's messages for future generations.

ELIJAH

One of the most influential prophets to the northern kingdom of Israel was Elijah. Elijah was famously taken to heaven in a chariot of fire. Over 850 years later, Elijah reappeared along with Moses on a high mountain to talk with Jesus. This special event is known as the transfiguration of Christ because eyewitnesses saw Jesus' face shine like the sun and his clothes became white like light.

▶ *This statue of Elijah is on Mount Carmel in northern Israel.*

PROPHETS AND SCRIBES

Many prophets were scribes. Some prophets, like Jeremiah, had scribes of their own. Jeremiah's scribe, Baruch, wrote down the prophet's words on a scroll and read them aloud to the people.

▶ *This seal belonged to Baruch, the scribe of Jeremiah the prophet.*

▶ *Picture of a scribe.*

◀ *Hezekiah tore down houses in Jerusalem and used the stones to build this twenty-foot thick wall as a defense against the invading armies of Sennacherib, King of Assyria.*

▶ *Isaiah told King Hezekiah that God would move the shadow backwards ten steps on the stairway as a sign that his prophecy would come true.*

SENNACHERIB'S PRISM

Sennacherib, King of Assyria, recorded his military campaigns on six-sided clay prisms. On one side, he records the siege of Jerusalem. He says "As for Hezekiah the Judahite … he himself I shut up in Jerusalem, his royal city, like a bird in a cage." As we know today, that's all that happened. God did not allow the Assyrian army to conquer Judah but sent them back home as Isaiah prophesied.

IMPORTANT MESSAGE

This picture shows King Hezekiah dying. Isaiah visited the king with a special message. Isaiah said God promised to heal Hezekiah and deliver Jerusalem from the Assyrians by sending King Sennacherib back to his own land.

◀ *Twenty-one letters written on clay were found in the ruins of the city of Lachish. These provide details about King Nebuchadnezzar's attacks and the destruction of the temple in Jerusalem in 586 BC. Pieces of pottery used to write letters are called ostraca.*

Did You Know?

You've probably heard the story of Jonah. Could this have actually happened? Whether the story of the fish can be proven or not, we do know God, in his great love, sent Jonah to Nineveh, the capital city of the Assyrian empire. The people in this city were Israel's fierce enemies. After hearing Jonah's message, 120,000 people, including the king, repented and turned to God.

▲ *Jonah may have sailed on a vessel such as this model of a sixth century BC merchant ship from Greece.*

Kingdoms rose and fell in Old Testament Bible times. Eventually, in 586 BC, Jerusalem was destroyed. The once-magnificent temple was burned to the ground. It was tragic, however God raised up prophets like Daniel and Ezekiel as examples of faith and with messages of hope.

TIMES OF SORROW

Ezekiel lived in Jerusalem until 597 BC. That's when Nebuchadnezzar exiled 10,000 more captives including Ezekiel and members of the royal family. Those were sad years in Israel. But the prophet Ezekiel promised Israel that God would one day return them to their own land.

▶ *This is a picture of what Jerusalem may have looked like when it fell in 586 BC.*

SECRET NIGHTMARES

King Nebuchadnezzar, the Babylonian king, had bad dreams that he wanted explained. None of the wise men could help so he went to Daniel. Daniel prayed and asked God to reveal both the secret dreams and their meaning. God told Daniel that Nebuchadnezzar's dream was about a gigantic statue with a golden head, bronze belly, iron legs, and feet of iron and clay. The dream, Daniel explained to the king, was about the kings of the earth and the governments of the end times. Nebuchadnezzar said, "Surely your God is the God of gods and the Lord of kings." Then he promoted Daniel to rule over the entire province. Daniel also was appointed the chief administrator of Babylon's wise men.

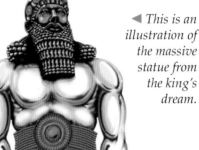

◀ *This is an illustration of the massive statue from the king's dream.*

◀ *Captives from Judah were forced to travel far away from their homeland and live as exiles in Babylon.*

MAGNIFICENT GATE

The two majestic towers of the Ishtar Gate stood forty feet tall. Archaeologists have rebuilt this gate that once welcomed visitors to the temples of Babylon.

Mediterranean Sea
Euphrates R.
Tigris R.
Riblah
ISRAEL
Babylon
Jerusalem
BABYLONIAN
JUDAH
EMPIRE

0   200 km.
0   200 miles

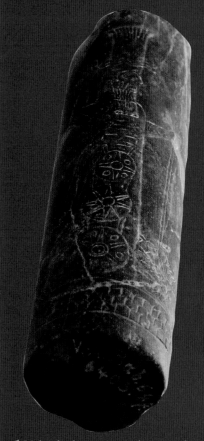

Did You Know?

King Nebuchadnezzar issued a decree—everyone must worship the golden statue of his god. Three young Hebrew men refused to bow down to the 90-foot image. Their punishment? They were thrown into the flames of a fiery furnace. But the flames didn't even hurt them. King Nebuchadnezzar instantly proclaimed a new decree. Everyone must honor the God of the Hebrews. To learn more about the three Hebrews read, Daniel 3:1–30.

◄ *Written in cuneiform, this fragment records the details of Babylonian history, including Nebuchadnezzar's conquest of Jerusalem in 598 BC.*

◄ *This gold cup from ancient Persia remind us of the ones Belshazzar drank from at his feast.*

FALL OF THE EMPIRE

After Nebuchadnezzar died, King Belshazzar took over. One day he held a fantastic feast. He called for the gold and silver goblets that King Nebuchadnezzar had taken from the temple in Jerusalem. As they drank wine from those holy cups, everyone praised the gods and idols of Babylon. Suddenly, the fingers of a human hand appeared and wrote a message on the wall. Terrified, no one could interpret the writing. Daniel was called in. He told the king that God was pronouncing judgment against him. That very night, King Belshazzar was killed. The Babylonian empire came to an end. It was taken over by Darius the Mede.

◄ *Nebuchadnezzar may have made an enormous statue of this Babylonian god named Marduk.*

MYSTERIOUS MESSENGERS

From Genesis to Revelation, angels are busy at work. Some are mighty warriors; others are messengers, appearing to people to pronounce warnings or to announce births. Angels are divided into two main groups. There are good angels who are loyal to God and help people. There are evil angels who rebelled against God and tempt people to do wrong things. The Bible explains that these "fallen angels" cause torment, pain, and wickedness on the earth. The Bible shows how the good angels are sent by God to guide people, guard them from danger, and help them in times of need.

▲ Ivory cherubim carving from Samaria.

ENCOURAGERS

When Jesus was in the Garden of Gethsemane the night before he was crucified, he was in extreme anguish. He was getting ready to take the punishment for the whole world's sins. The Bible says an angel appeared to Jesus in the garden and strengthened him.

▲ The angel Gabriel told Mary she would be the mother of Jesus.

GABRIEL, THE MESSENGER

The angel Gabriel appears several times in the Bible as a messenger. Gabriel appeared to Daniel while he was living in Babylon and helped him understand visions he had. Gabriel was also sent to Zechariah with the message that he would have a special child. This child grew up to be John the Baptist. Gabriel was also sent to tell Mary that she would have a baby even though she was not yet married. Her son would be named Jesus, who was the promised Messiah.

◄ This image portrays Michael, chief of the good angels, conquering Satan, chief of the wicked angels.

MICHAEL, THE ARCHANGEL

The angel Michael is one of the most important angels mentioned in the Bible. He is an archangel, one of the chief princes of the angels and the commander of God's army of heavenly hosts. When war broke out in heaven Michael led his army against the army of evil angels. The devil and his wicked angels were cast down to earth and lost their place in heaven.

DANIEL IN THE LIONS' DEN

Because of his faith in God and refusal to worship any other gods, Daniel was thrown into a den of lions. God sent his angel to shut the mouths of the lions. The next morning, Daniel was lifted out of the den, safe from harm.

VISIONS AND ANGELS

While in exile in Babylon, the prophet Ezekiel saw many visions of angels. In his writings, he tried to describe some of what he saw. One type of angel, called seraphim, looked like a person but had four faces. It had the face of a person, the face of a lion, the face of an ox, and the face of an eagle. These angels also had four wings. Under their wings they had human hands. Many artists have tried to draw angels based on the description Ezekiel gave.

Did you know?

When the Israelites built the tabernacle, they decorated some of the curtains with pictures of cherubim. Years later King Solomon carved the doors and the walls of the temple with figures of cherubim. To learn more about angels, read Revelation 4:1–5:14.

▶ *The curtains on this model of the tabernacle are decorated with cherubim, angels with wings.*

Great changes occurred throughout the land after Cyrus the Great conquered the Babylonian empire. Most notable was the decree that allowed captive Israelites to return to Jerusalem. Once there, they started rebuilding the temple and the holy city. It was not an easy task. Governors and local leaders bullied them and even tried to organize assassination attempts. These setbacks only made the Jews pray harder and work with even greater devotion to their people, their city, and their God. After many years and through the reign of different Persian kings, the second temple was completed and the wall surrounding Jerusalem was rebuilt.

PURIM

The festival of Purim celebrates how Esther bravely asked King Xerxes to stop Haman's wicked plan to destroy all the Jews.

DANGEROUS TIMES

Xerxes I reigned over the Persian Empire after Darius. He chose Esther, the brave and beautiful Jewish maiden, as his queen. It was during this time that Haman, a high-ranking official, asked the king to kill all the Jews. Not knowing the queen and her loyal cousin Mordecai were Jews, Xerxes issued the decree.

◄ *Elaborate Persian drinking vessel.*

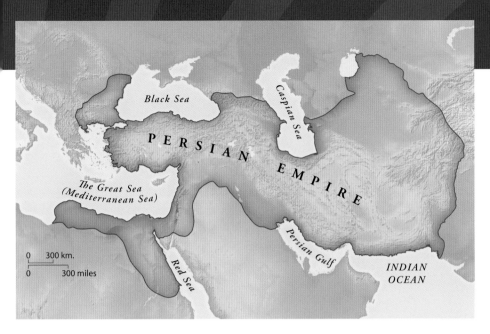

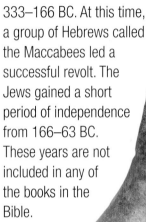

◄ *After conquering the Babylonians in 539 BC, Cyrus the Great ruled over the powerful new Persian Empire.*

END OF THE PERSIAN EMPIRE

After two centuries, the Persian Empire was conquered by Alexander the Great from Greece. The Greek empire then ruled the land from 333–166 BC. At this time, a group of Hebrews called the Maccabees led a successful revolt. The Jews gained a short period of independence from 166–63 BC. These years are not included in any of the books in the Bible.

CYRUS CYLINDER

The Cyrus Cylinder is a record of Cyrus the Great's conquest of Babylon. It explains how exiles captured by the Babylonians were then allowed to return home and rebuild their temples. The Jews carried with them 5,400 treasures of silver and gold that Nebuchadnezzar had looted from the temple in Jerusalem. They also brought with them permission from King Cyrus to rebuild the temple.

▶ *Bronze helmets such as this one were worn by troops in the battles between the Greeks and the Persians.*

▶ *Gold daric coin with Darius, King of Persia, as a hunter.*

A NEW DECREE

After King Cyrus died, Darius stepped into the line of Persian kings. Earlier, the Jews had been building the temple but their enemies forced them to stop. King Darius issued a new decree: Allow the Jews to finish their work on the holy temple in Jerusalem. Use money from the royal treasuries to pay them daily for anything they needed. Finally, the second temple of Israel would be finished.

Did You Know?

When Jerusalem was destroyed in 586 BC, the city's walls were knocked down. Nehemiah led the returning exiles to rebuild the protective walls surrounding the holy city. To learn more about Nehemiah, read Nehemiah 2:1–18.

▶ *Archaeologists have excavated part of the Jerusalem wall built under the leadership of Nehemiah.*

Rome ruled the vast lands surrounding the Mediterranean Sea. While the empire had good roads, marketplaces filled with life's necessities and luxuries, theaters and palaces, and advanced technology for things such as aqueducts, the people of Israel felt oppressed. They were not able to worship God as they wanted. Many longed for their promised Messiah to come and free them from the grip of Rome.

THE SYNAGOGUE

In New Testament times, the synagogue was a central part of Jewish life. Every Saturday, Jewish families honored the Sabbath, the holy day of rest, when they went to their local synagogue. Men would read from scrolls containing the writings of the Torah (the first five books of the Old Testament). On holidays and feast days people celebrated at the synagogue. It was also where young boys went to Hebrew school. This synagogue near the Sea of Galilee dates back to the time of Jesus.

SYNAGOGUE SCHOOLS

Like other young children, Jesus probably would have attended Hebrew school at his local synagogue, called a bet-sefer. Their teacher, called a sofer, would have taught them to read and write Scripture.

◀ *Jesus' name in Hebrew is Yeshua, which means "to save, deliver." Hebrew is written and read from right to left.*

HOUSES

Houses varied throughout the Roman Empire. Most people rented apartments and had to share bathing and kitchen facilities. For a regular family, furniture and decorations were simple: ordinary furniture such as tables, chairs, and beds were made of wood. Wealthy families may have built more extravagant homes with several levels. Floors could have pretty stone designs called mosiacs. Furniture might be fancier, using marble or bronze with wood.

◀ *The scrolls of the Torah were kept in a beautiful box called an ark. Each synagogue had its own ark and scrolls which scribes copied carefully.*

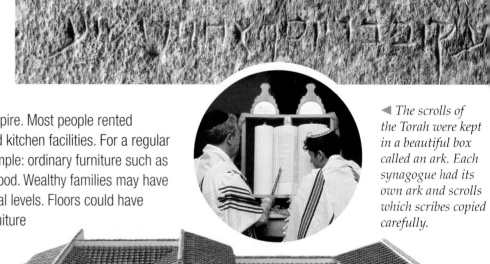

▶ *Model of an artistic rendition of a home owned by a wealthy citizen in Jerusalem.*

◄ Carpenter at his workbench.

CARAVANS FROM AFAR

Merchants traveled in caravans of camels and donkeys bringing their produce from far away to sell in the local marketplaces. Jewelry, papyrus, and unique foods arrived from all over the Roman Empire, such as Egypt, Babylonia, and Greece.

OCCUPATIONS

Many people in New Testament times were farmers and grew grains. Others were herders with flocks of sheep and goats. There were also many skilled workers and craftsmen. Joseph, the adoptive father of Jesus, was a carpenter. As his son, Jesus learned the carpenter's trade as well.

Many different coins were used in Israel and all throughout the Roman Empire.

▼ Denarius—Roman coin

Did you Know?

Except for the wealthy who ate on low couches like the Romans, many Jewish families enjoyed their meals sitting around a mat spread out on the floor. Food was placed in the center. A bowl of food was served to each member of the family.

▶ Tetradrachma— Greek coin equal to four Roman denarius

▲ Lepton— Jewish coin of small value ▶

TRUMPETS, FEASTS, AND HOLY DAYS

Holidays held special meaning for the Jews. Each was a very holy day, a time to draw close to God, remember his blessings, and honor the sacred Scriptures. Around 1250 BC, when Moses led the Hebrews out of Egypt, God gave the Israelites detailed instructions on how to celebrate important feasts and holy days. Moses wrote these instructions in the book of the covenant, and devout Jews were to follow the instructions very carefully.

▲ *For the first Passover in Egypt, the Hebrews were instructed to kill a lamb and spread its blood on the sides and tops of their doors so the angel of death would pass over their house and not kill their firstborn son.*

EYEWITNESS ACCOUNT

Josephus was a Jewish historian who lived around the same time as Jesus. He wrote about Jewish and Roman history. He gave an eyewitness account of the great number of Israelites who visited the temple in Jerusalem each year during the feasts. He said, "And indeed, at the feast of unleavened bread, which was now at hand, and is by the Jews called the Passover, and used to be celebrated with a great number of sacrifices, an innumerable multitude of the people came out of the country to worship." About 30,000 people lived in Jerusalem at this time. Scholars estimate that between 100,000 and 300,000 Jews visited the holy city during the Pilgrim Feasts.

▲ *This ancient sign found in the Temple Mount instructs the priests to go "to the place of the trumpeting."*

▲ *The shofar or ram's horn could be heard in Jerusalem calling the people to gather for a sacred assembly or holy feast day.*

PASSOVER FEAST

During Passover each year, crowds swelled the streets of Jerusalem. Many families camped in the fields around the city. Each family visited the temple. They presented a Passover lamb as a sacrifice for the forgiveness of their sins. The priest sprinkled the lamb's blood on the altar to show that God forgave their sins. Then the meat was given back to the family. Returning to their campsite, they ate the Passover meal. This meal was a special time to remember how God saved their people from the tenth plague long ago when they were slaves to Pharaoh.

▲ *Shavuoth, Festival of First Fruits, celebrated the start of the spring barley harvest.*

FEAST OF TABERNACLES

The Feast of Tabernacles (or Booths) was a joyous time to remember the close presence of God and how God was with Moses and the Israelites in the wilderness. Families built shelters called sukkot out of branches and palm fronds. They ate and even slept inside sukkot such as this one.

FEAST OF TRUMPETS

The holy day of the Feast of Trumpets (or Rosh Hashanah) was announced with horns and trumpet blasts.

◄ *The feast of Purim celebrated when the Jews were saved from Haman's evil plot to kill all the Jews. Today, it is a happy time when children dress up to retell the story.*

FEAST OF UNLEAVENED BREAD

The Feast of Unleavened Bread celebrated when God brought the Hebrew ancestors out from Egypt and established them as the nation of Israel.

Did You Know?

Hanukkah is also known as the Feast of Dedication (or Festival of Lights). In 164 BC, a Jewish family named the Maccabees had rededicated the temple after it was defiled by the king of Syria. According to tradition, Judah Maccabee found a small amount of oil that was only enough to last for one day. Miraculously, however, it provided enough light for eight whole days. During New Testament times, every Jew, including Jesus, celebrated this feast. To learn about what happened when Jesus visited the temple at Hanukkah, read John 10:22–42.

WHERE IS THE NEWBORN?

A group of mysterious travelers arrived in Jerusalem. They had come from far away in the east, perhaps from Susa or Babylon. They went straight to Herod the Great, king over the region. They asked him where they could find the newborn King of the Jews. Herod assembled the chief priests and scribes and demanded to be told where the Messiah was supposed to be born. The teachers of the law explained that the prophet Micah said the king would be born in Bethlehem.

THE MOST WONDERFUL NIGHT OF ALL

The night of Jesus' birth was very exciting! Angels appeared above the fields outside Bethlehem praising God. When they left, the shepherds hurried into Bethlehem. They saw the newborn Son of God just as the angel said. Then they spread the news to everyone they knew.

◄ *Many families display a nativity set in their home to remember the wonderful night Jesus was born.*

AN IMPORTANT BIRTH

Because of the census, Joseph and Mary had to leave their home in Nazareth. They traveled to Bethlehem, a village just south of Jerusalem, because they were descendants of King David. When they arrived in Bethlehem, the time came for Mary to give birth to her son.

▼ *King David and his descendant Jesus were both born in Bethlehem.*

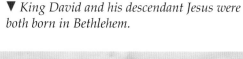

◄ *Emperor Caesar Augustus ruled the Roman Empire, including Israel, from 31 BC to AD 14. He ordered everyone in the Roman world be counted in a census. Each family had to return to the hometown of their ancestors to register.*

STARGAZERS

The cuneiform writing on this planisphere from seventh-century BC Assyria gives information about the constellations and positions of stars. Wise men in Persia may have studied such writings. It is not known what religion the magi who visited Jesus followed. Perhaps they were descendants of Daniel or other Hebrews exiled in Babylon.

◄ *According to the Law of Moses, mothers without much money could bring either a pair of doves or two pigeons as an offering because they had just given birth to a son.*

ACCORDING TO THE LAW

Mary and Joseph were careful to follow the Law of Moses concerning baby Jesus. He was taken to the temple in Jerusalem and consecrated to God as Mary's firstborn son. The new parents offered a traditional sacrifice.

TIME OF FEAR AND SORROW

When King Herod heard about an infant king, he ordered Roman soldiers to kill every boy in Bethlehem two years old or younger. Joseph, however, escaped to Egypt with Mary and Jesus. Their journey may have taken them through the barren wilderness like in this painting.

Did You Know?

Even though the Bible does not say how many wise men followed the star to Jesus, it does list the three gifts they gave. Gold was a royal gift fit for a king. Frankincense was used to worship God in the temple. Myrrh was a spice used when wrapping a person's body after he dies. To learn more about the magi, read Matthew 2:1–12.

► *This map shows the route Joseph and Mary probably took from Nazareth to Bethlehem to Egypt and then back to Nazareth where Jesus grew up.*

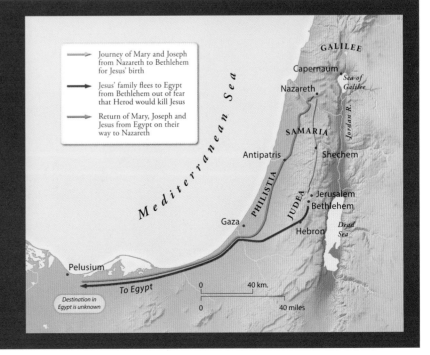

Journey of Mary and Joseph from Nazareth to Bethlehem for Jesus' birth

Jesus' family flees to Egypt from Bethlehem out of fear that Herod would kill Jesus

Return of Mary, Joseph and Jesus from Egypt on their way to Nazareth

GALILEE

Capernaum

Sea of Galilee

Nazareth

Mediterranean Sea

Jordan R.

SAMARIA

Antipatris

Shechem

PHILISTIA

JUDEA

Jerusalem
Bethlehem

Gaza

Dead Sea

Hebron

Pelusium

To Egypt

Destination in Egypt is unknown

0   40 km.

0   40 miles

Jesus chose twelve common men to be his disciples. These men studied Scriptures with Jesus and learned important lessons about God while they walked and talked with him. For three years these twelve lived with Jesus as constant companions and close friends. Two of these disciples, Matthew and John, went on to write historical accounts of Jesus' life and mission.

▲ *As Jesus and his followers walked from village to village, they may have worn sandals such as this 2,000-year-old pair found in the region of the Dead Sea.*

THE GALILEE BOAT

In 1986 the water level in the Sea of Galilee dropped drastically due to a two-year drought. Two brothers were walking along the shore when they saw a large object buried in the mud. Further investigation revealed the wooden structure of a very old boat. Specialists were called in to study it. They strengthened the water-soaked wood with wax-like chemicals so they could lift it out of the ground. Then they tested it with a process called Carbon-14 dating. They found this boat was 2,000 years old. It's often called the Jesus Boat because it dates from 100 BC–AD 70, around the same time Jesus sailed in similar boats with his disciples.

FISHERS OF MEN

One day as Jesus walked along the shore of the Sea of Galilee, he saw fishermen, brothers Simon, Peter, and Andrew, casting their nets into the water. He called to them, "Come, follow me, and I will send you out to fish for people." They left their nets and followed Jesus. From there, they saw two more brothers, James and John, repairing their nets. Again, Jesus called them to follow him and they did. At least four and perhaps seven of the twelve disciples (also known as apostles) were fishermen on the Sea of Galilee.

▶ *This map of the Sea of Galilee and its surrounding regions shows where the 2,000-year-old Galilee Boat was found in the mud.*

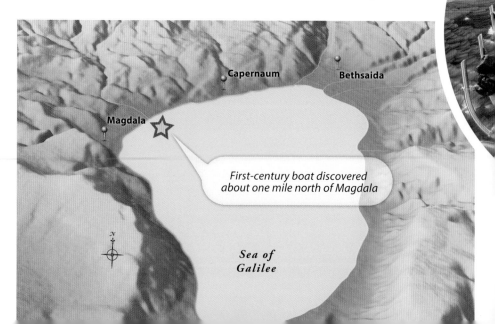

Capernaum

Bethsaida

Magdala

First-century boat discovered about one mile north of Magdala

Sea of Galilee

N

ANCIENT SYNAGOGUE

The black foundation at the ruins of this synagogue in Capernaum dates back to Jesus' time. It may have been a synagogue where Jesus and his disciples worshiped. The white walls are from a newer synagogue built on the site in the sixth century AD.

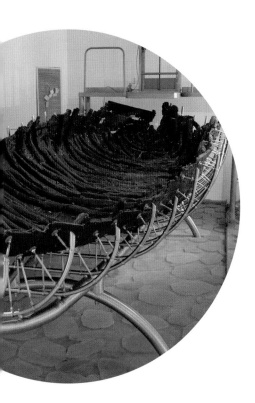

▲ *The Galilee Boat, now on display at the Yigal Allon Center, only a few miles from where it was found.*

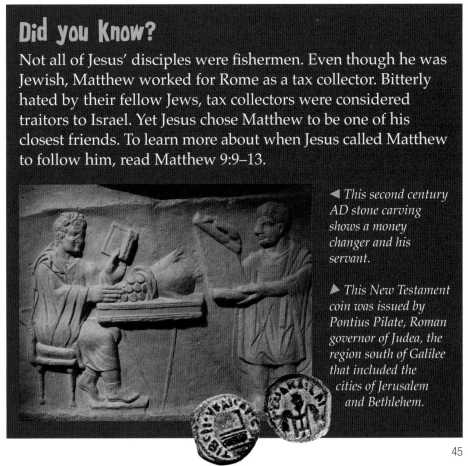

Did you Know?

Not all of Jesus' disciples were fishermen. Even though he was Jewish, Matthew worked for Rome as a tax collector. Bitterly hated by their fellow Jews, tax collectors were considered traitors to Israel. Yet Jesus chose Matthew to be one of his closest friends. To learn more about when Jesus called Matthew to follow him, read Matthew 9:9–13.

◀ *This second century AD stone carving shows a money changer and his servant.*

▶ *This New Testament coin was issued by Pontius Pilate, Roman governor of Judea, the region south of Galilee that included the cities of Jerusalem and Bethlehem.*

COULD HE BE THE ONE?

In New Testament times, many of the Jews were looking for the Messiah. They were hoping the Savior would come and save them from Roman oppression. Therefore, there was a common question among the crowds: "Could Jesus be the Messiah we're looking for?" Hundreds of people followed Jesus and watched his ministry. After listening to the lessons he taught and seeing the things he did, many people came to believe Jesus was the Messiah. Not everyone believed, however. Many key Jewish religious leaders did not approve of Jesus at all.

▼ *A map of Jesus' ministry.*

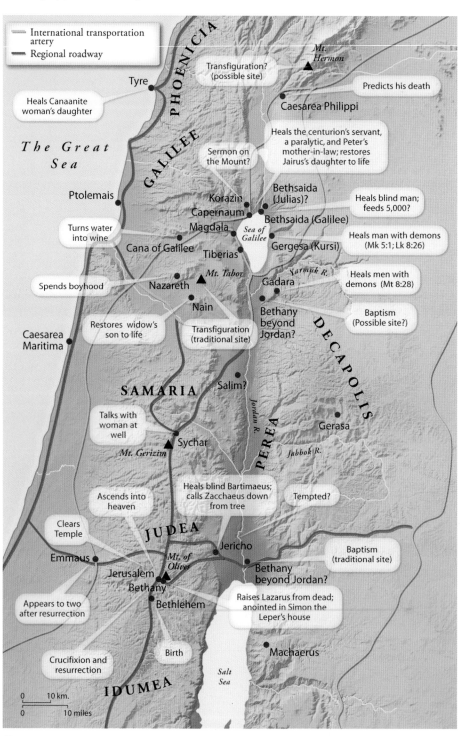

- International transportation artery
- Regional roadway

PHOENICIA

Tyre

Heals Canaanite woman's daughter

The Great Sea

Transfiguration? (possible site)

Mt. Hermon

Predicts his death

Caesarea Philippi

GALILEE

Sermon on the Mount?

Heals the centurion's servant, a paralytic, and Peter's mother-in-law; restores Jairus's daughter to life

Ptolemais

Korazin

Bethsaida (Julias)?

Heals blind man; feeds 5,000?

Capernaum

Bethsaida (Galilee)

Turns water into wine

Magdala

Sea of Galilee

Heals man with demons (Mk 5:1; Lk 8:26)

Cana of Galilee

Tiberias

Gergesa (Kursi)

Mt. Tabor

Yarmuk R.

Spends boyhood

Nazareth

Gadara

Heals men with demons (Mt 8:28)

Nain

Bethany beyond Jordan?

Baptism (Possible site?)

Caesarea Maritima

Restores widow's son to life

Transfiguration (traditional site)

DECAPOLIS

SAMARIA

Salim?

Talks with woman at well

Jordan R.

PEREA

Gerasa

Sychar

Mt. Gerizim

Jabbok R.

Heals blind Bartimaeus; calls Zacchaeus down from tree

Tempted?

Ascends into heaven

Clears Temple

JUDEA

Jericho

Baptism (traditional site)

Emmaus

Mt. of Olives

Bethany beyond Jordan?

Jerusalem

Bethany

Appears to two after resurrection

Bethlehem

Raises Lazarus from dead; anointed in Simon the Leper's house

Crucifixion and resurrection

Birth

Machaerus

Salt Sea

IDUMEA

0   10 km.
0   10 miles

▼ *Many people still visit the Jordan River to be baptized just as Jesus did.*

JOHN THE BAPTIST

Jesus' cousin, John, preached to the people and called them to turn away from sin and turn to God. Many people repented, and John baptized them in the Jordan River. One day, Jesus came to the Jordan River and wanted to be baptized too. John didn't want to baptize him but Jesus insisted, "Let it be so now; it is proper for us to do this to fulfill all righteousness." (John 3:15) So John baptized him.

JACOB'S WELL

One day Jesus spoke with a woman at Jacob's well in Samaria. Jesus told her all about her past and who she was. When she heard him say these things, she knew only the Messiah could know things like that. Jesus assured her that she was speaking to the Messiah! She was so excited, she called everyone from her village to come meet Jesus. After meeting him, many Samaritans chose to believe Jesus was the Messiah.

▲ *On the walls of the Church of the Pater Noster in Jerusalem, the Lord's Prayer is written in 140 languages.*

SERMON ON THE MOUNT

Large crowds followed Jesus. One day Jesus decided to teach a special lesson. He climbed up onto this mountainside. Then he began to speak about God. The words he spoke became known as the Sermon on the Mount.

THE LORD'S PRAYER

During the Sermon on the Mount, Jesus taught the people how to pray. Today this is called the Lord's Prayer.

TEMPTATION AND TESTING

After Jesus was baptized, the Holy Spirit led him into the wilderness where he fasted and prayed for 40 days and nights. Satan came to tempt Jesus, testing him with promises of riches and power. But Jesus did not allow himself to be tempted.

THE TRANSFIGURATION

This mosaic on the ceiling of the Church of the Transfiguration shows the Transfiguration, when Jesus' face shone like the sun and his clothes dazzled white as light. Moses and Elijah appeared to talk with him as Peter, James, and John looked on.

Did You Know?

When Jesus taught, he often used examples the people could easily understand and relate to. Jesus told the crowds that he is the Good Shepherd. He said he takes excellent care of his sheep because he loves them. To learn more about Jesus, the Good Shepherd, read John 10:1–18.

TEACHING WITH PARABLES

When Jesus spoke to the crowds, he often told stories called parables. Each of the parables taught an important lesson. Some parables taught about the kingdom of God. Others taught about topics such as prayer, love, or God's judgment. Still other parables taught lessons about doing good works.

PARABLE OF THE SOWER

This twelfth-century picture above illustrates the parable of the sower, the farmer who planted seeds. This story tells how some seeds fell in places they did not grow. Other seeds fell on good soil and grew to produce a large crop. This parable taught people to be like seeds in good soil and produce lots of good fruit.

◄ This story is about a woman who had ten coins and lost one. She lit a candle, swept the house, and searched carefully. When she found it, she called all her friends and neighbors to rejoice with her. This parable teaches how everyone in heaven rejoices when one sinner repents.

PARABLE OF THE MUSTARD SEED

In this parable, Jesus compared the kingdom of God to the tiny mustard seed. A mustard plant grows tall and birds nest in its branches. This parable taught the lesson that great things can grow from small beginnings, like Jesus' ministry did.

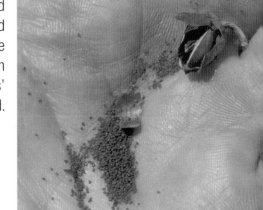

WORKERS IN THE VINEYARD

In this parable, the owner of a vineyard paid all the workers the same amount no matter how many hours they worked. This lesson taught about God's mercy and grace. God gives salvation to all who ask for it, not because of works they might do.

THE LOST SON

Often called the Parable of the Prodigal Son, this story is about a wealthy father whose son leaves home and wastes his money doing bad things. When he realizes things cannot get any worse, the son goes back home and asks his father to forgive him. The father welcomes his son home, gives him a big hug, and throws him a party. This parable teaches about God the Father's great love and forgiveness for all.

◄ *When he was away from home, the lost son became so hungry he ate carob pods such as these that were fed to the pigs.*

PARABLE OF THE WEDDING FEAST

In this parable, a king prepares a wedding banquet for his son. The people he invites refuse to attend, so he invites anyone who will come. This parable teaches that God invites everyone to be saved, but only those who accept this invitation and choose to repent will live in heaven with him.

► *In Bible times, wedding feasts lasted for seven days.*

PARABLE OF THE WHEAT

Jesus told a story about a farmer who planted wheat. An enemy snuck in and planted weeds in the same field. This parable taught that while Jesus' followers live on earth, Satan will be working evil here as well.

Did You Know?

One of the most famous parables Jesus told is the Good Samaritan. In this story, robbers beat a man who was traveling to Jericho. They left him beside the road almost dead. First a Jewish priest passed by. Then a Levite. Neither of them stopped. But Jesus said a Samaritan man stopped to help the traveler, taking him to an inn and paying someone to care for him. What lesson did this parable teach? Love your neighbor as yourself. To learn more about this parable, read Luke 10:25–37.

▲ *This ancient inn is along the same road to Jericho as in the parable of the Good Samaritan.*

There was something different about Jesus. He taught with great authority, performed miracles, and even raised people from the dead. Because of his miracles, many people believed Jesus was the Messiah. But many others did not. Filled with rage, some groups of religious leaders tore their robes each time Jesus claimed to be God. In their opinion, this was blasphemy.

▶ *This map shows the region of Galilee where Jesus performed his first public miracle.*

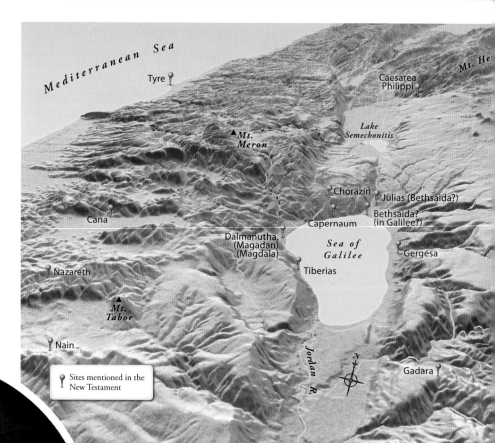

Mediterranean Sea

Tyre

Caesarea Philippi

Mt. He[...]

Mt. Meron

Lake Semechonitis

Cana

Chorazin

Julias (Bethsaida?)

Bethsaida? (in Galilee?)

Capernaum

Dalmanutha, (Magadan) (Magdala)

Sea of Galilee

Gergesa

Nazareth

Tiberias

Mt. Tabor

Nain

Jordan R.

Gadara

Sites mentioned in the New Testament

STORM

Once, when the disciples sailed with Jesus across the Sea of Galilee, a fierce storm threatened to drown them. Jesus commanded the storm to stop. Instantly, all was still. Who was this man named Jesus? Even the winds and waves obeyed him.

FIRST MIRACLE

Jesus attended a wedding in Cana with his disciples. His mother Mary and his brothers were there too. When the host ran out of wine, Mary told Jesus. Jesus told the servants to fill six stone jars with water. When they served it to the guests, they realized Jesus had turned the water into wine. Because of this first miracle, his disciples began to believe in him.

ANCIENT MANUSCRIPT

Matthew, Mark, Luke, and John are the books of the Bible known as the Gospels. Two of them, Matthew and John, are eyewitness reports of Jesus' work. Shown here is the earliest fragment in existence of the Gospels. Part of the book of John dates back to about AD 125–130.

▲ *This shows the tomb of Lazarus today.*

THE TOMB OF LAZARUS

Jesus' friend Lazarus had died. By the time Jesus got there, Lazarus had been buried for four days. When he arrived, Jesus stood at the tomb opening and shouted, "Lazarus, come out!" Everyone was shocked to see Lazarus walk out of the tomb, still wrapped in strips of cloth.

THE TEMPLE TAX

Peter came to Jesus concerned about paying the temple tax. Jesus told Peter to go fishing and catch a fish. What did Peter find inside the fish's mouth? A four-drachma coin, enough to pay the tax for both Jesus and Peter.

◀ *Perhaps the fish Saint Peter caught was this kind of fish, a tilapia.*

SABBATH TROUBLE

This is a model (left) of the twin pools of Bethesda. It was here, on the Sabbath, that Jesus healed a man unable to walk for 38 years. Jesus told the invalid to pick up his mat and walk. So the man did. It was against the Jewish law for anyone to carry a mat on the Sabbath, however. So when the Jewish leaders heard about this they were furious Jesus had done this good deed on the Sabbath.

Did you Know?

All four Gospels record the miracle of Jesus feeding a crowd of 5,000 with just five loaves of bread and two fish. When finished, they gathered twelve baskets of leftovers.

ENTER THE GATES OF THE HOLY CITY

God had promised to send his Son, the Messiah, to save the world. Jesus knew this was his purpose on Earth. He had been telling his disciples to prepare for it. Jesus joined the crowds going to Jerusalem for the Passover. He went right into the hands of the chief priests and Pharisees who had put out an order for his arrest.

EYEWITNESS REPORT

Matthew wrote in his gospel about the day Jesus entered Jerusalem just before Passover. Matthew said that as Jesus drew near to the holy city, he began to weep over it. Jesus felt sad that many of his own people did not recognize him as their Messiah.

▲ *Model of Jerusalem*

HEROD THE GREAT

The Jerusalem in Jesus' day was heavily influenced by Herod the Great, the king when Jesus was born. Herod had gone to great expense to build projects throughout the city. These included his own palace, the Fortress of Antonia, and a Greek-style theater. Herod's crowning glory was the reconstruction and expansion of the magnificent Jewish temple.

◄ *Here we see the western wall of the temple area in the ancient city of Jerusalem.*

▲ *This is a view of Herod's palace, located across the city to the west of the temple.*

Did You Know?

The crowds in Jerusalem heard Jesus was coming into the city, riding on a donkey's colt. They cut palm branches and hurried out to greet him. "Hosanna!" they shouted, throwing their branches on the ground before him. Others spread their cloaks on the road. "Blessed is the king of Israel!" they cried. Today this important event is celebrated as Palm Sunday. To learn more about what happened on this special day, read Matthew 21:1–17.

▲ *Modern Palm Sunday celebration in Jerusalem.*

HEROD'S TOMB

Herod the Great died in 4 BC. The land of Israel was divided among his sons. This picture below shows the Herod family tomb in Jerusalem.

ROMAN GARRISON

King Herod built the Antonia Fortress, a huge barracks where Roman troops lived in the city of Jerusalem. It was located right next to the temple so soldiers could keep an eye out for any trouble that might threaten Rome's rule.

▼ *This 1892 painting by Enrique Simonet shows Jesus weeping over Jerusalem.*

THE DARK DAY

It was the year AD 30. Rome ruled the world. Yet in the streets of Jerusalem many repeated the name of Jesus. The chief priests and leaders of the Jews were horrified. Roman soldiers were removing any threat to their emperor, Caesar. So what if Rome heard about this man Jesus? Would they tear down the temple and destroy Jerusalem and the Jewish nation? The leaders of the Jews decided it was time for action.

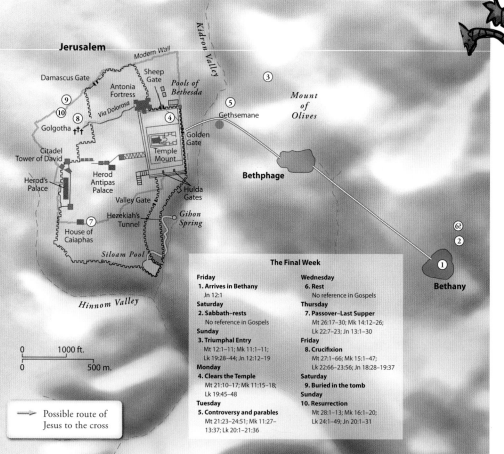

Jerusalem

Modern Wall
Kidron Valley
Damascus Gate
Sheep Gate
③
Antonia Fortress
Pools of Bethesda
⑨
Via Dolorosa
⑤
Mount of Olives
⑩ ⑧
Gethsemane
Golgotha ✝✝✝
④
Golden Gate
Citadel Tower of David
Temple Mount
Bethphage
Herod's Palace
Herod Antipas Palace
Valley Gate
Hulda Gates
House of Caiaphas
Hezekiah's Tunnel
Gihon Spring
⑦
⑥?
②
Siloam Pool
①
Bethany
Hinnom Valley

0   1000 ft.
0   500 m.

→ Possible route of Jesus to the cross

The Final Week

Friday	**Wednesday**
1. Arrives in Bethany	**6. Rest**
Jn 12:1	No reference in Gospels
Saturday	**Thursday**
2. Sabbath-rests	**7. Passover–Last Supper**
No reference in Gospels	Mt 26:17–30; Mk 14:12–26;
Sunday	Lk 22:7–23; Jn 13:1–30
3. Triumphal Entry	**Friday**
Mt 12:1–11; Mk 11:1–11;	**8. Crucifixion**
Lk 19:28–44; Jn 12:12–19	Mt 27:1–66; Mk 15:1–47;
Monday	Lk 22:66–23:56; Jn 18:28–19:37
4. Clears the Temple	**Saturday**
Mt 21:10–17; Mk 11:15–18;	**9. Buried in the tomb**
Lk 19:45–48	**Sunday**
Tuesday	**10. Resurrection**
5. Controversy and parables	Mt 28:1–13; Mk 16:1–20;
Mt 21:23–24:51; Mk 11:27–	Lk 24:1–49; Jn 20:1–31
13:37; Lk 20:1–21:36	

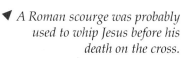

◀ *A Roman scourge was probably used to whip Jesus before his death on the cross.*

◀ *This map shows the places where key events took place in Jerusalem during the last days of Jesus.*

A SPECIAL GARDEN

After the Passover meal, Jesus took 11 of his disciples to a nearby olive grove called the Garden of Gethsemane. While the men slept, Jesus spent the night in prayer. Jesus knew it was God's will that he go to the cross. An angel appeared who strengthened Jesus. He stood up and called his disciples. The time had come.

◀ *The olive groves at the traditional site of Gethsemane has trees that are 900 years old.*

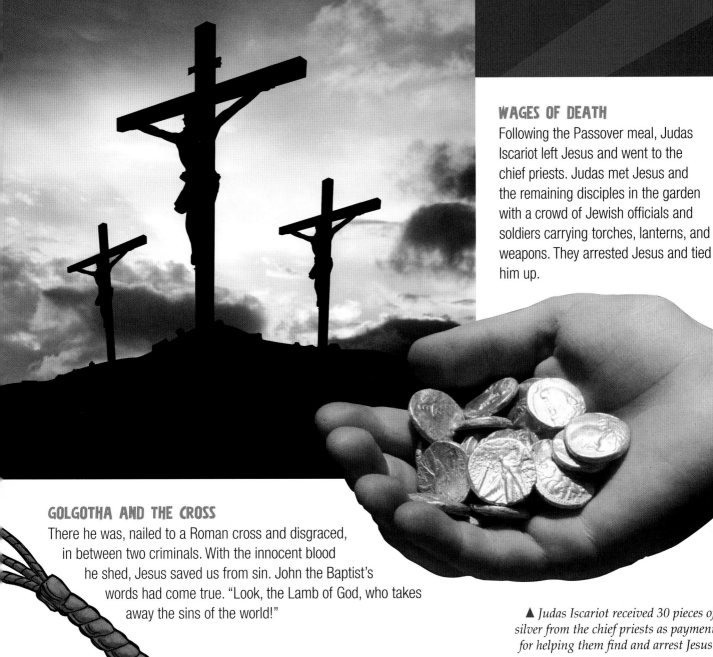

WAGES OF DEATH

Following the Passover meal, Judas Iscariot left Jesus and went to the chief priests. Judas met Jesus and the remaining disciples in the garden with a crowd of Jewish officials and soldiers carrying torches, lanterns, and weapons. They arrested Jesus and tied him up.

GOLGOTHA AND THE CROSS

There he was, nailed to a Roman cross and disgraced, in between two criminals. With the innocent blood he shed, Jesus saved us from sin. John the Baptist's words had come true. "Look, the Lamb of God, who takes away the sins of the world!"

▲ *Judas Iscariot received 30 pieces of silver from the chief priests as payment for helping them find and arrest Jesus.*

Did You Know?

Jesus ate the Passover meal with his disciples. Today this is known as the Last Supper. Many believers today participate in a ceremony called communion during which they eat bread and sip wine or grape juice to remember Jesus, the Last Supper, and his sacrifice on the cross.

GARDEN TOMB

Pilate gave permission for Joseph of Arimathea to bury Jesus. According to tradition, this was Joseph's own tomb.

LIES, RUMORS, AND HOPE

It was three days since Jesus had been crucified and buried. Pilate had given strict orders that the tomb be sealed, so a heavy stone was placed across the entrance. Guards were stationed to keep watch. But now what was going on? All that was left was an empty tomb.

TRUTH OR LIE?

On Easter morning, some of the guards at Jesus' tomb ran to the chief priests and told them Jesus was gone. The chief priests paid the guards to spread the lie that the disciples stole the body of Jesus. When the women and other followers arrived at the tomb, it was empty—but an angel told them the truth. Jesus had risen from the dead.

◄ *This ancient tomb has a large circular stone to roll across its entrance to keep wild animals and thieves away.*

MOUNT OF OLIVES

After continuing to teach his disciples, and instructing them to spread the Gospel to the world, Jesus returned to heaven after forty days. Jesus and his disciples gathered at the Mount of Olives. While his followers watched, Jesus was taken up to heaven. This is called the Ascension.

Did you Know?

On the day Jesus was crucified, Nicodemus took a mixture of burial spices to anoint Jesus' body. A man of great wealth, he had about 75 pounds of myrrh and aloes to use to wrap the body in strips of linen according to Jewish burial customs.

TALKING WITH JESUS

After meeting the women near the tomb, Jesus appeared to two of his followers walking along the road to Emmaus. The men did not recognize Jesus until they sat down to eat a meal together. Then Jesus disappeared. The men were so excited they immediately hurried back to Jerusalem to tell the others. When they got there they discovered that Jesus had also appeared to Peter.

EAST GATE

Jerusalem's East Gate was sealed shut by Arabs in medieval times to try to stop Jesus from coming back. This was because the prophet Ezekiel prophesied the Messiah would one day return to the temple through the gate facing east.

GREAT JOY

Early in the morning, on the third day after Jesus was crucified, Mary Magdalene, Jesus' mother Mary, and Joanna brought more spices to anoint the body of Jesus. Instead, they found Jesus resurrected from the dead. They fell at his feet and worshiped him with joy. Jesus greeted them and said, "Do not be afraid. Go and tell my brothers to go to Galilee; there they will see me."

THE MESSIAH

The disciples weren't scholars of the Scriptures like the Jewish elders were. So while on earth Jesus taught them about all the Old Testament Scriptures and prophecies concerning the Messiah. Jesus showed them how he fulfilled each one. During the forty days he was on earth after the resurrection, Jesus appeared to his followers and taught them even more. Then he told them to wait in Jerusalem for the gift of the Holy Spirit. They would be given power to teach what they learned to the world.

SON OF DAVID

God promised King David that the Messiah would be one of his descendants. (Psalm 89:3–4) Jesus was born into King David's royal line. (Luke 3:23–38)

▶ Illuminated version of Jesse's Tree—the family tree of Christ beginning with Jesse and his son King David.

BY THE SEA OF GALILEE

When he began his ministry, Jesus lived in Capernaum near the Sea of Galilee. This fulfilled the prophet Isaiah's words: "But in the days to come he will honor Galiee, where people from other nations live. He will honor the land along the Mediterranean Sea. And he will honor the territory east of the Jordan River." (Isaiah 9:1–2)

◀ View of excavations of the ruins of Capernaum. The synagogue where Jesus preached is in the background.

BORN IN BETHLEHEM

The prophet Micah said the Messiah would be born in Bethlehem. (Micah 5:2) Jesus was born in Bethlehem where he was laid in a manger. (Luke 2:1–7 and Matthew 2:1–8)

▲ *Stone manger found at Megiddo.*

CALLED A NAZARENE

An unknown prophet said the Messiah would come from the city of Nazareth. Jesus returned from exile in Egypt with his family and grew up in Nazareth. (Matthew 2:19–23)

► *Remains of a 1st century house discovered in Nazareth with the Church of the Nativity in the background.*

BORN OF A VIRGIN

The prophet Isaiah said the Messiah would be born of a virgin. (Isaiah 7:14) Mary, the mother of Jesus, was a virgin and not yet married when she became pregnant with Jesus through the power of the Holy Spirit. (Luke 1:26–38)

Did You Know?

King David said the Messiah would have zeal for God's house. (Psalm 69:9) Once, when Jesus went to the temple, he found people selling cattle and sheep in the courts as if it were a marketplace. Jesus made himself a whip and drove them all out. To learn more about Jesus and his zeal for the temple, read John 2:13–17.

At the time Jesus ascended to heaven, there were about 120 believers including Mary, the mother of Jesus, Jesus' brothers, the 11 remaining disciples, and Matthias, the man chosen to replace Judas. They stayed in an upper room in Jerusalem and waited, just as Jesus said to.

PENTECOST

It was Pentecost. Jews from all over the Roman Empire had traveled to Jerusalem to celebrate. Coming fifty days or seven weeks after the Passover, this feast was also known as the Festival of Weeks. Devout Jews brought offerings to the temple. According to tradition, this was also a celebration of the day Moses received the Ten Commandments.

▲ *This room is traditionally thought to be near the original site of the upper room where the early church first met.*

BIRTH OF THE CHURCH

On the day of Pentecost, the believers were gathered together in the upper room. Suddenly the sound of a violent wind roared down from heaven and filled the house. Fire appeared in the air. It separated, and a tongue of fire rested on each one of the believers. All of them were filled with the Holy Spirit. They began to speak about the wonders of God in different languages they did not know. The noise was so loud that crowds of people came running. Jews from all over the empire heard God being praised in their own language. Peter stood up and explained how Jesus was the Messiah and had baptized them that day with the power of the Holy Spirit. About 3,000 more Jews were baptized that day. To learn more about Pentecost read Acts 2:1–12.

► *The Sanhedrin was a group of Jewish leaders who met in Jerusalem and acted as a court of law.*

High Priest

Accused

35 members

35 members

Clerk

Clerk

Stud seat

JOSEPHUS ON JAMES

The Jewish historian Josephus tells how James, the brother of Jesus and a leader in the early church, was martyred around AD 61. This was done by the high priest Ananus, a member of the Sadducees. In his writings, Josephus said that Ananus "assembled the Sanhedrin of judges, and brought before them the brother of Jesus, who was called Christ, whose name was James, and some others, [or, some of his companions]; and when he had formed an accusation against them as breakers of the law, he delivered them to be stoned."

▲ *Two letters Peter wrote became part of the New Testament. Shown is a copy of the second letter, dated from about AD 200.*

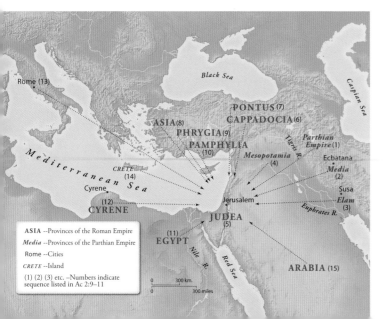

Rome (13)

Black Sea

PONTUS (7)

CAPPADOCIA (6)

ASIA (8)

PHRYGIA (9)

PAMPHYLIA (10)

Parthian Empire (1)

Mesopotamia (4)

Caspian Sea

Ecbatana

Media (2)

Susa

Elam (3)

Mediterranean Sea

CRETE (14)

Cyrene

(12)
CYRENE

Jerusalem

JUDEA (5)

Euphrates R.

(11)
EGYPT

Nile R.

Red Sea

ARABIA (15)

ASIA --Provinces of the Roman Empire
Media --Provinces of the Parthian Empire
Rome --Cities
CRETE --Island
(1) (2) (3) etc. --Numbers indicate sequence listed in Ac 2:9–11

0   300 km.
0   300 miles

▲ *This Dominican monastic complex, just outside the Jerusalem Old City walls, was built in the 4th century and dedicated to Stephen.*

FIRST MARTYR

The Jewish leaders thought they had gotten rid of Jesus. But now his followers were carrying on his ministry. Miraculous healings. Powerful teachings. Excited crowds. The apostles were arrested, jailed, and beaten. But they would not stop. Finally, the Jewish leaders seized a man named Stephen. They put him on trial before the Sanhedrin. Taking matters into their own hands, they stoned Stephen to death.

Did You Know?

Peter was staying in Joppa in a house probably a lot like this one. One day he went up on the roof to pray. While there he received a vision that resulted in him going to Caesarea to share the Gospel with a man named Cornelius. To learn more about the miraculous events that happened, read Acts 10:1–48.

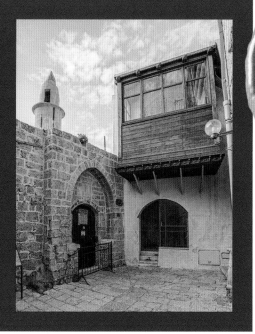

EXTREME PERSECUTION

This coin shows the profile of Nero, the fifth emperor of Rome. Christians suffered cruel and horrible persecution under his rule, including both Peter and Paul, leaders of the early church.

The Jews flocked to Jerusalem to worship at their beloved temple. But with the rise of the Roman Empire, Jerusalem was no longer just the holy city of the Jews. It became a powerful stronghold for Roman rule. Herod built his palace within Jerusalem so he could reign over the city. He constructed the mighty Fortress Antonia so he could quickly stop any religious uprising against Rome. For entertainment, he built a gigantic Roman theater and a racetrack.

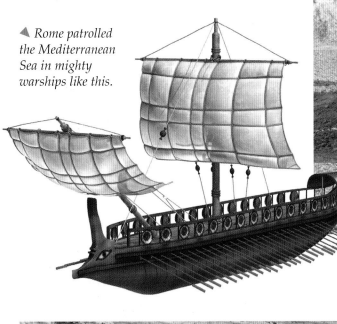

◄ *Rome patrolled the Mediterranean Sea in mighty warships like this.*

▲ *This is a replica of a Roman catapult used about AD 67.*

► *A Roman charioteer races his team of horses to the finish line on this oil lamp.*

ARCH OF TITUS

In Rome, the Arch of Titus was built to celebrate the fall of Jerusalem. A giant menorah being carried through the streets of Rome during the victory parade is carved on the arch.

THE TEMPLE DESTROYED

In AD 70, the Roman general Titus destroyed Jerusalem and set fire to the temple. Today you can still see the huge boulders that were thrown down and landed on the southwest side of the Temple Mount. They are a reminder of Jesus' prediction: "Do you see all these great buildings? Not one stone here will be left on another; every one will be thrown down." (Matthew 24:2)

CAESAREA MARITIMA

To bring the Roman world to Judea, Herod the Great needed a protected harbor. He built a harbor at Caesarea Maritima along the coast of the Mediterranean Sea. Huge blocks of concrete were piled up to create a breakwater so ships could safely dock. Trade ships arrived carrying exotic goods from North Africa, Spain, and Rome. Thanks to Herod's design, the city also had a sewer system, aqueducts, and magnificent buildings rivaling those in Rome.

Did you Know?

Roman rule had become unbearable. Jews began to revolt against the Roman rule. They seized control of Jerusalem and established a Jewish government. Soon Roman troops marched in to take back the land for Caesar.

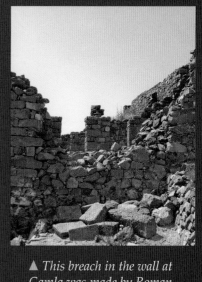

▲ *This breach in the wall at Gamla was made by Roman soldiers in AD 66.*

HIPPODROME

The Romans loved games. Herod built a Roman hippodrome in a valley south of the Temple Mount to accommodate this love. Cheering crowds gathered there to watch charioteers race around the track as well as gladiator games.

THOSE IN CHARGE

In New Testament times, there were three main groups of Jewish leadership: the Pharisees, the Sadducees, and the Essenes. The most important group was the Pharisees. They developed an extensive list of traditions and oral laws that were not written in the original Law of Moses. The Sadducees were wealthy priests who came from upper-class families. They only followed the written Law of Moses. The Essenes were the smallest group and usually lived together in close-knit communities. They followed very strict rules of their own and mostly did not marry. Many scholars think the Essenes lived near the caves at Qumran and created the Dead Sea Scrolls.

FLAVIUS JOSEPHUS

Born in Jerusalem about AD 37, Josephus was a Jewish historian. He was an eyewitness to significant events in first-century Israel. His writings provide a valuable resource for Jewish history.

◄ *Josephus was a priest and a member of the Pharisees.*

▲ *These are the Huldah Gates located at the southern end of the Temple Mount. The Sanhedrin probably entered the temple through these gates. Both Pharisees and Sadducees were members of the Sanhedrin.*

WESTERN (WAILING) WALL

Jesus predicted the destruction of the temple even though it happened 40 years after his death and resurrection. This section of the foundation of the western wall in Jerusalem is all that was left. Previously called the Wailing Wall, it is a place many people visit for prayer and open mourning for the destruction of the Temple.

DOME OF THE ROCK

The once magnificent temple was destroyed by Romans in AD 70. Some people claim a rectangular hole carved into the rock bed is where the Ark of the Covenant once stood inside the temple. This rock bed is inside the Dome of the Rock, a Muslim shrine built on the Temple Mount.

▲ *Jewish pools for ceremonial bathing are called mikveh.*

RITUAL BATHS

These steps led down to a pool at the southern end of the Temple Mount. Religious washings and purification ceremonies took place in these underground baths. Priests took a ritual bath before participating in their temple duties.

▲ *This box, called an ossuary, held the bones of Caiaphas, high priest in the Sanhedrin, during the trial of Jesus. Caiaphas was a Sadducee.*

▲ *The courtyard in front of the temple is where the priests officiated over the sacrifices and offerings.*

Did You Know?

With over 6,000 members, the Pharisees were the largest and most influential group of Jewish leaders. They complained that Jesus and his disciples did not follow all the Jewish traditions. To learn more about what Jesus said to the Pharisees, read Matthew 23:1–39.

STRANGE IDOLS AND PRISON CELLS

Saul, a leading Jewish Pharisee, didn't like that the early church was growing stronger. Saul arrested followers of Jesus in Jerusalem. He gained permission from the high priest to go to the city of Damascus and do the same. He didn't want any changes to Jewish traditions. But something happened. When Saul showed up in Damascus, he said he was a believer in Jesus Christ! Saul was a changed man. Even his name changed to Paul. Now a Christ-follower, missionary, and writer of letters in the Bible, Paul set out to change the world.

▲ *This painting of Paul dating from AD 300 was found in a cave near Ephesus.*

EPHESUS AND IDOL INDUSTRY

A great deal of Paul's ministry was in Ephesus. Ephesus was a center for the worship of the idol Artemis. A magnificent temple of Artemis stood in this city. One day a violent riot against Paul and the Christians broke out at the theater. Demetrius, a silversmith, accused Paul of ruining the idol-making business that used to flourish in Ephesus. So many Gentiles had become Christians that hardly anyone bought idols anymore.

ROMAN CITIZEN

Paul was born a Roman citizen. It was a privilege and honor not everyone had—it had to be earned and the road was not easy. For example, the sailor mentioned in the writing on this piece of bronze (above) from AD 79 didn't receive this certificate of Roman citizenship until he served 25 years in the Roman navy.

▲ *It was here at Antioch in Syria that the followers of Christ were first called Christians.*

ANTIOCH

Several years after Paul became a believer, Barnabas asked Paul to join him in the city of Antioch to help teach the Scriptures to these new believers, who were mostly Gentiles.

DANGEROUS JOURNEYS

Paul's three missionary journeys were dangerous. In many cities, leading Jews stirred up violent crowds against Paul. When he healed a lame man in Lystra, Paul was stoned until they thought he was dead. At Philippi, Paul and Silas were arrested, beaten, and thrown in jail. In spite of these difficulties and more, Paul and his fellow missionaries planted new churches, trained people to lead them, and continued to spread the good news of salvation through Jesus Christ.

Did You Know?

Saul set off for Damascus to arrest members of the early church. Suddenly, a bright light flashed down from heaven. Blinded, Saul fell to the ground. Jesus appeared to him and spoke. Then Saul was led into the city to a house on Straight Street where he received his sight back and joined the church. To learn more about Paul's conversion, read Acts 9:1–31.

▲ *Paul and Silas were possibly chained in this jail in the city of Philippi where, through a series of miraculous events, the jailer and his entire family became Christians.*

◄ *Artemis in Ephesus.*

▲ *Straight Street is still in Damascus.*

▼ *This platform in Corinth was the bema, or judgment seat, where Paul stood trial.*

CORINTH AND JERUSALEM

Paul and fellow missionaries such as Timothy, Titus, Silas, Aquila, and Priscilla established a church in the Greek city of Corinth located about 50 miles from Athens. It was here that Paul was brought before the judgment seat of Rome. Gallio, proconsul of the region, refused to declare Paul guilty of a crime and let him go. This important legal decision gave Paul permission to continue his ministry in Corinth. At the end of his third missionary journey, Paul left Corinth and headed back to Jerusalem.

SHIPWRECKS AND CAESAR

By the end of Paul's third missionary journey, he had one goal in mind: Get to Jerusalem to celebrate Pentecost. God warned Paul that prison awaited him. His friends warned Paul he would be captured by the Jews and handed over to the Gentiles. But he knew God wanted him to share the good news of Jesus Christ. He put his life in God's hands.

TEMPLE RIOT

Paul arrived in Jerusalem with Luke. They met with James, Peter, and the other apostles. The leaders of the Christian church rejoiced to hear about the ministry of Paul among the Gentiles. A few days later Paul was at the temple. He was dragged out and the temple gates were shut. The Jews tried to kill him. But Roman troops raced to the scene, arrested Paul, and bound him in chains.

▶ Paul was shipwrecked while sailing in a boat similar to this cargo ship.

AN APPEAL TO CAESAR

Paul was locked in prison for two years at Caesarea. He appeared on trial before various rulers including Felix, the Roman governor, and King Agrippa II, great-grandson of Herod the Great. Under death threats from the Sanhedrin, Paul finally declared, "I appeal to Caesar!" Festus, the Roman governor pronounced, "To Caesar you will go!" So Paul was sent to Rome on a cargo ship that was battered by a terrible storm and was shipwrecked on the island of Malta.

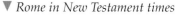

▼ Rome in New Testament times

APPIAN WAY

Finally, Paul and his companions reached Rome. Christian believers from the church at Rome came out to greet them. They walked along this road, the Appian Way. Encouraged by their warm welcome, Paul shared his testimony with them and invited them to visit.

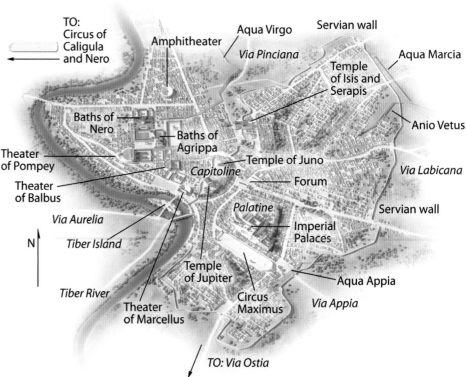

MAMERTINE PRISON

It was here in the dungeon of the Mamertine prison that Paul suffered in jail for the last time. He died in Rome, a martyr, about AD 67.

PERSECUTION FROM ROME

Nero reigned as Caesar from AD 54–68. Paul appeared on trial before him in AD 63 and was probably released from custody at that time. In AD 64, a fire burned Rome down. Nero was accused of starting the fire himself. To take the blame off his own shoulders, he pointed his finger at the Christians. With this, he started a persecution of Christians. According to tradition, Nero had both Paul and Peter killed for their faith.

Did you Know?

At first Paul was imprisoned in Jerusalem, probably at the Antonia Fortress. It was too dangerous to keep him in Jerusalem, however. So Paul was secretly sent by night to Caesarea, shown here in this photograph. Two hundred Roman soldiers, 70 horsemen, and 200 spearmen guarded Paul along the journey. When he arrived in Caesarea he was placed under guard in Herod's palace. To learn more about Paul's arrest and imprisonment, read Acts 23:1–35.

WRITING THE REST OF THE BIBLE

The Bible speaks to us about Jesus Christ and the history of the early church. But the Bible is not just a history book. It is also a book of faith. So how did the Bible come to us today? Who made it possible for us to read what people wrote 2,000 years ago and what Moses wrote over a thousand years before that?

◀ *Because of his beliefs, John was exiled as a prisoner here on the island of Patmos when he wrote the book of Revelation.*

LETTERS AND VISIONS

The apostle Paul wrote letters to the churches he established. James, Jude, Peter, and John also wrote letters to groups of Christians. Along with these, it is generally accepted that the disciple John wrote the book of Revelation based on visions he had. All these writings from the early church leaders, along with the Gospels and Acts, were written in Greek.

◀ *Written in Greek on parchment, the Codex Sinaiticus is the oldest surviving complete manuscript of the New Testament. It also contains part of the Old Testament.*

CODEX

In the second century AD, Christians began to copy Scripture on flat sheets. Christians would fold the sheets and fasten the pages together on the side. Called a codex, this format was easier to carry and read than a bulky scroll.

▲ *This relief shows a group of Romans reading scrolls. The original books of the Bible were written on scrolls.*

NEW TESTAMENT SCRIBES

For over a thousand years, the books of the New Testament were copied by hand. After Emperor Constantine legalized Christianity, more and more scribes made copies of the Bible. By the 11th century AD, most monasteries and abbeys had their own scribes.

▶ *John wrote in Revelation that Jesus will return to Jerusalem as a conquering king.*

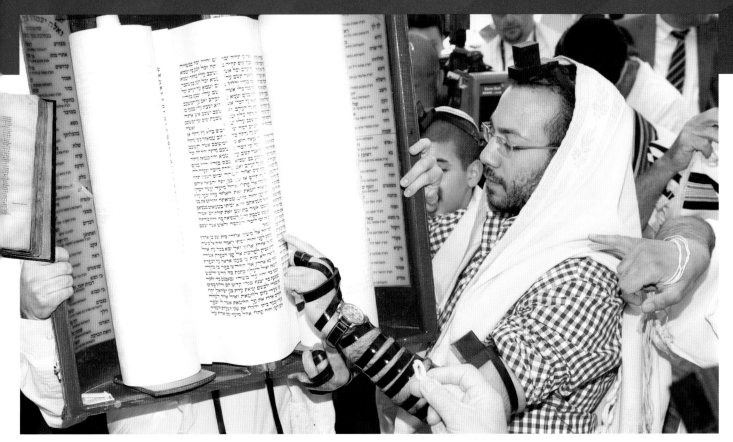

▲ *Devout Jew reading a scroll of the Torah.*

FIRST ENGLISH TRANSLATION

John Wycliffe (1330–1384) believed every person should be able to read the Bible.

At this time, only Latin translations were available. Wycliffe decided to translate the Bible himself, along with his friend Nicholas Purvey. Commoners in England who could not read Latin rejoiced to receive Wycliffe's English version of the Bible.

◄ *Only 170 copies of the complete Wycliffe Bible (and 25 copies of the original) are still in existence today.*

HEBREW BIBLE

In Jesus' day, there were three kinds of Scriptures: the Law, the Prophets, and the Writings. The Law, or Torah, included Genesis through Deuteronomy. The Prophets included Joshua through 2 Kings and prophets such as Isaiah and Jeremiah. The Writings included some documents written at a later time. All these Scriptures from the Hebrew Bible are the same 39 books in the part of the Christian Bible known as the Old Testament.

Did You Know?

In 1611, a group of more than 50 scholars released the King James Bible. Backed by King James I of England, its purpose was to accurately translate Scripture into English. Although many new translations and interpretations have been published since 1611, the King James Bible is the most popular translation of the Bible.

> it not be knowen, that a woman came into the floore.
>
> 15 Also he said, Bring the ‖ vaile that thou hast vpon thee, and holde it. And when she helde it, he measured sixe measures of barley, and laide it on her: and he went into the citie.
>
> 16 And when shee came to her mother in law, she said, Who art thou, my

THE BIBLE IN ITS TIME

Period of the judges
Judges–1 Samuel 8
1380–1050 BC

Creation
Gen. 1–2
Dates unknown

Fall
Gen. 3
Dates unknown

Flood
Gen. 6–8
Dates unknown

2000 BC   1800 BC   1600 BC   1400 BC   1200 BC

Jacob and family move to Egypt
Exod. 1
Dates unknown

The Hebrew people conquer Jericho
Josh. 6
1406 BC

Abraham
Gen. 12–25
2166 BC

The exodus, Red Sea crossed
Exod. 12
1446 BC

King David
2 Sam. 2–24;
1 Chron. 11–29
1010–970 BC

Birth of Christ
Matt. 1–2;
Luke 1–2
6/5 BC

Life, death, and resurrection of Christ
Matthew–John
AD 26–30

Ministry of the apostle Paul
Acts–Philemon
AD 46–68

The book of Revelation written
Revelation
AD 95

1000 BC   800 BC   600 BC   400 BC   200 BC

Fall of Israel (northern kingdom)
2 Kings 17
722 BC

Nehemiah rebuilds the walls
Nehemiah
432 BC

Roman Empire conquers the land of Israel
63 BC

Fall of Judah (southern kingdom)
2 Kings 25
586 BC

Aaron: The brother of Moses, first high priest of Israel.

Abraham: Father of the Jewish nation, he moved from Ur to the Promised Land where God made a covenant to bless him and bless all nations through him.

Adam and Eve: The first man and woman, they disobeyed God and brought sin and death into God's perfect creation.

Ahab: Wicked king of Israel, he married Jezebel and tried to change the official religion to the worship of Baal.

Boaz: Son of Rahab and Salmon, he was a kinsman of Ruth and the great-grandfather of King David.

Daniel: Carried into captivity by Nebuchadnezzar, he was appointed to high positions because of his wisdom and gift for interpreting dreams.

David: A young shepherd from Bethlehem who became the second and most famous king of Israel, he was an ancestor of Jesus Christ.

Deborah: Prophetess and judge of Israel, she held court under a palm tree where people came to her to settle their arguments.

Delilah: Beautiful Philistine woman, she tricked Samson into telling her the secret to his strength.

Elijah: Great prophet of Israel, he fought against the worship of Baal. He was carried to heaven in a chariot of fire.

Elisha: Following Elijah as the next prophet in Israel, he ministered through the rule of six different kings.

Esther: Jewish maiden married to the Persian king Xerxes. The holiday of Purim celebrates how she bravely protected her people from a plot to destroy all the Jews.

Ezekiel: Jewish prophet living in exile at Babylon.

Ezra: Priest and scribe, he led a group of exiles from Babylon back to Jerusalem and worked with Nehemiah to teach their people the Law of Moses.

Gabriel: Important angel, he delivered messages to Daniel and later announced the births of John the Baptist and Jesus Christ.

Gideon: One of the judges of Israel, he led a military campaign against the Midianites.

Haggai: Prophet, he encouraged the Israelites to rebuild the temple in Jerusalem.

Hagar: Egyptian servant to Sarah, she gave birth to Abraham's son Ishmael.

Hannah: Mother of Samuel, she dedicated her son to the Lord.

Hezekiah: A king of Judah, he led the Hebrews in a nationwide reform to return to God.

Hosea: Prophet in Israel, his marriage was an example of the unfaithful relationship of Israel toward God, and God's forgiveness and love for his people.

Isaac: The son of Abraham and Sarah, he and his wife Rebekah gave birth to twin sons, Esau and Jacob.

Isaiah: A major prophet who lived in Jerusalem, he prophesied the coming Messiah.

Ishmael: Abraham's son born to him by Sarah's maidservant Hagar.

Jacob: The son of Isaac and Rebekah whose name was changed to Israel, his twelve sons became the twelve tribes of Israel.

Jeremiah: Prophet of Judah, he ministered during the final stages of the Babylonian empire's conquest of Jerusalem.

Job: A strong man of faith, he went through a time of great suffering to become even closer to God.

Jonah: Prophet who was swallowed by a great fish, he later delivered a message of repentance to the city of Nineveh.

Joseph: Sold into slavery by his brothers, he rose to be second in command under Pharaoh and saved his own family from famine.

Joshua: The assistant of Moses who went on to lead the Israelites to the Promised Land.

Josiah: King of Judah who found the book of the law, he went on to lead his people back to God.

Leah: Jacob's first wife, she is known as one of the mothers of the twelve tribes of Israel.

Malachi: Prophet around the time of Nehemiah. His book is the last book in the Old Testament.

Michael: Known as an archangel, he led the faithful angels against Satan and his wicked angels.

Miriam: A prophetess, she was the sister of Moses and Aaron.

Mordecai: Esther's cousin and guardian, he counseled her as queen to step forward and do her part to overturn the plot to destroy the Jews.

Moses: Brought up in the courts of Pharaoh, Moses lead the Hebrews out of Egypt, delivered the Ten Commandments, built the Tabernacle, and guided the Hebrews to the Promised Land.

Nehemiah: A governor of the Jews, he led his people to rebuild the wall around Jerusalem.

Noah: The one man declared righteous on the earth in ancient times, he built an ark to save his family and the animals from a worldwide flood sent to wipe out sin.

Queen of Sheba: Ruler of an ancient land, she traveled to Jerusalem to witness the wealth, power, and wisdom of King Solomon.

Rachel: Jacob's second wife, known as one of the mothers of the twelve tribes of Israel.

Rahab: Canaanite who lived in the city wall of Jericho, she joined the Hebrew faith, married and had a son named Boaz, and was an ancestor of Jesus Christ.

Rebekah: Wife of Isaac, the mother of twin sons Esau and Jacob.

Ruth: Widow from Moab who joined the Hebrew faith. She moved to Bethlehem where she married Boaz and had a son who was the grandfather of King David.

Samson: Judge of Israel, famous for his strength, he delivered his nation from the Philistines.

Samuel: The last judge of Israel and one of its first prophets, he anointed both Saul and David as kings of Israel.

Sarah: Mother of the Jewish nation, she married Abram and had a son named Isaac in their old age.

Saul: First king of Israel, he was replaced by David because of his disobedience toward God.

Shadrach, Meshach, and Abednego: Three young Hebrew men who served King Nebuchadnezzar in Babylon.

Solomon: King David's son. While king, he built the temple in Jerusalem and was famous for his great wisdom.

WHO'S WHO IN THE NEW TESTAMENT

Ananias and Sapphira: Early Christians in Jerusalem, this husband and wife lied about the amount of money they were donating to the church only to die.

Andrew: Brother of Peter and a fisherman, he was one of Jesus' 12 disciples.

Anna: Elderly widow who worshiped at the temple day and night, she told others how she saw the newborn Jesus when his parents brought him to the temple.

Aquila and Priscilla: Tentmakers by trade, this husband and wife team were friends and co-workers of Paul in the early church.

Barnabas: Jewish believer from Cyprus, he invited Paul to work with him in the early church at Antioch, and he traveled with Paul on his first missionary journey.

Bartimaeus: Blind beggar at the gates of Jericho, he was healed by Jesus.

Caesar Augustus: Ruler of the Roman Empire after the death of Julius Caesar, he ordered the census that sent Joseph and Mary to Bethlehem where Jesus was born.

Caiaphas: High priest during the mock trial of Jesus by the Sanhedrin, he persecuted the members of the early church.

Cleopas: One of two disciples walking on the road to Emmaus, the resurrected Jesus appeared to him and his companion.

Cornelius: Roman centurion stationed at Caesarea, he invited Peter to share the gospel with him, becoming Peter's first Gentile convert.

Crispus: Jewish leader of the synagogue in Corinth, he became a Christian after hearing Paul preach.

Dorcas: Raised back to life by Peter, her important ministry was sewing clothing for the needy.

Epaphras: A founder of the church at Colossae, he visited Paul in Rome where he was thrown in jail.

Eutychus: A young man who fell asleep in his third-story window seat while listening to Paul preach, he fell to the ground and died, but Paul restored him to life.

Herod the Great: Cruel ruler of Judea during the time of Jesus' birth, he ordered all the infant boys murdered in Bethlehem in his effort to assassinate the newborn king.

James: Brother of Jesus, he became the leader of the church in Jerusalem and wrote the book of James in the Bible.

James: Brother of John, he was the first of the 12 disciples to be martyred for his faith.

Jesus Christ: Born of a virgin named Mary, he is the Messiah, the Savior of the World.

John: Brother of James, he was one of the 12 disciples and is credited with writing the Gospel of John, three letters in the Bible, and probably Revelation.

John the Baptist: Cousin of Jesus, he prepared the crowds for the ministry of Jesus by calling them to repent and be baptized. He also baptized Jesus.

Joseph: A descendant of King David and a carpenter, he married Mary the mother of Jesus.

Joseph of Arimathea: Wealthy member of the Jewish Sanhedrin, he buried the body of Jesus in his unused tomb.

Judas Iscariot: One of the 12 disciples, he betrayed Jesus to the leading priests in Jerusalem for 30 pieces of silver.

Jude: Brother of Jesus, he became a leader in the early church and wrote the book of Jude.

Lazarus: Close friend of Jesus and a brother to Mary and Martha, Jesus raised him from the dead.

Luke: A physician by profession, he was a close companion of Paul on his journeys and wrote the Gospel of Luke and Acts.

Lydia: Wealthy merchant who sold purple cloth from her region, she became a Christian and opened her home as a headquarters for Paul and the church in Philippi.

Mark: Young nephew of Barnabas, he worked at times under some controversy with Paul and wrote the Gospel of Mark.

Martha: Sister to Lazarus and Mary of Bethany, she served various times as hostess to Jesus and his friends.

Mary, the Mother of Jesus: She joined the disciples and other believers in Jerusalem in the early days of the church.

Mary: Sister to Lazarus and Martha who is remembered for her acts of devotion toward Jesus. Shortly before his death, she anointed Jesus' feet with a costly perfume and wiped his feet with her hair.

Mary Magdalene: Part of a group of women who supported Jesus and his disciples with money and food, she was the first to see Jesus after he rose from the dead.

Matthew: Tax collector at Capernaum, he became one of the 12 disciples of Jesus and wrote the Gospel of Matthew.

Nicodemus: Pharisee and a member of the Sanhedrin, he was a secret follower of Jesus who helped with his burial.

Paul: Known as the apostle to the Gentiles, he preached to the Roman Empire on three missionary journeys, then wrote letters to the various churches he planted. A number of these letters became books in the Bible.

Peter: A fisherman from Galilee, he became one of the 12 disciples and a prominent leader of the early church.

Philemon: Wealthy member of the church at Colossae, Paul asked him to forgive his runaway slave who had become a Christian.

Philip: An evangelist and leader in the early church in Jerusalem, he was one of the men chosen to help look after the widows and elderly.

Phoebe: Well-to-do believer, Paul recommended her to the Christians at Rome as a kind and helpful friend.

Pontius Pilate: Roman governor of Judea, Jesus was brought on trial before him and was sentenced to death on the cross even though Pilate declared Jesus innocent.

Rhoda: Young woman in the home of Mark's mother, she answered the door when Peter escaped miraculously from jail but was so excited to share the news that she left Peter standing out on the street.

Salome: Mother of James and John from Galilee, she joined other women to support Jesus and his disciples with money and food.

Silas: Close friend and co-worker of both Peter and Paul, he traveled with Paul on his second missionary journey.

Simeon: Elderly and devout Jew, he held baby Jesus in his arms at the

temple and proclaimed this infant was the Messiah they'd been waiting for.

Stephen: A Greek-speaking Jew who was part of the early church in Jerusalem, he was the first Christian to be martyred for his faith.

Thomas: One of the 12 disciples, he did not believe Jesus had risen until he saw Jesus himself.

Timothy: A young convert from Lystra. Under Paul's training, he became a leader in the churches Paul had started in cities such as Berea, Thessalonica, Corinth, and Ephesus.

Titus: A Greek believer, he became one of Paul's closest and most influential co-workers.

Zacchaeus: Jewish tax collector in Jericho whose life was changed when he met Jesus. He is remembered for climbing a tree to catch sight of Jesus as he went through town.

Zechariah and Elizabeth: Parents of John the Baptist, Zechariah was a priest who served at the temple in Jerusalem two times each year.

PHOTO CREDITS

Voices in the Desert

Statue of Elijah on Mount Carmel	© Asaf Eliason/Shutterstock
Model of ancient Greek merchant ship	Z. Radovan/www.BibleLandPictures.com
Painting of Hezekiah in bed	Standard Publishing/Goodsalt
Jerusalem wall	© 1995 by Phoenix Data Systems
Sennacherib's prism	Wikimedia Commons
Carving of scribes	© by Zondervan
Seal of Baruch	Z. Radovan/www.BibleLandPictures.com
Lachish letters fragments	©2013 by Zondervan

Captives in a Foreign Land

Map of the exile from Judah	Map by International Mapping. Copyright © by Zondervan.
Replica of Ishtar Gate	© rasoulali/Shutterstock
Marduk	Kim Walton. The Pergamon Museum, Berlin.
Babylonian Chronicle	© Baker Publishing Group and Dr. James C. Martin. Courtesy of the British Museum, London, England.
Ancient Persian gold cups	© Baker Publishing Group and Dr. James C. Martin. Courtesy of the British Museum, London, England.
Painting of Jerusalem	© Lebrecht Music and Arts Photo Library/Alamy Stock Photo
Statue from Nebuchadnezzar's dream	Copyright ©2011 by Zondervan

Mysterious Messengers

Reconstructed tabernacle curtains	© Baker Publishing Group and Dr. James C. Martin.
Ivory cherubim	A. D. Riddle/www.BiblePlaces.com, taken at the Israel Museum
Angel from Ezekiel's vision	Plaque depicting Vision of Ezekiel, Mosane School, French School, (12th century)/Musee Dobree, Nantes, France/Bridgeman Images
Daniel in the lions' den	Copyright 2006 digitalartbytedlarson.com
Michael the archangel crushing Satan beneath his foot	Wikimedia Commons
The Annunciation	© Renata Sedmakova/Shutterstock
Jesus in Gethsemane	Wikimedia Commons

Decrees, Danger, and Devotion

Map of the Persian Empire	Map by International Mapping. Copyright © by Zondervan.
Cyrus cylinder	© 2013 by Zondervan
King Darius coin	A. D. Riddle/www.BiblePlaces.com
Stone carving of Xerxes	© Anton Ivanov/Shutterstock
Persian drinking vessel	Gold rhyton, Persian civilisation, Achaemenid dynasty, 5th-4th century BC/National Museum of Iran, Tehran/DeAgostini Picture Library/Bridgeman Images
Child dressed for Purim celebration	© Ekaterina Lin/Shutterstock
Nehemiah wall	Todd Bolen/www.BiblePlaces.com
Persian bronze helmet	Z. Radovan/www.BibleLandPictures.com

Everyday Life in New Testament Times

Ancient Galilee synagogue	www.HolyLandPhotos.org
Yeshua carved in stone	Paradiso/Wikimedia Commons, The James ossuary was on display at the Royal Ontario Museum from November 15, 2002 to January 5, 2003.
Scrolls of the Torah	Z. Radovan/www.BibleLandPictures.com
Model of a rich man's home at the time of Jesus	Todd Bolen/www.BiblePlaces.com
Traditional meal setting	A. D. Riddle/www.BiblePlaces.com
Carpenter's tools	Copyright © 2015 by Zondervan
Camel caravan	© Ahmad A Atwah/Shutterstock
Denarius	Jay King
Tetradrachma	Marie-Lan Nguyen/Wikimedia Commons, CC BY 2.5
Lepton	© Lee Prince/age fotostock

Trumpets, Feasts, and Holy Days

Temple instructions carving	Greg Schechter from San Francisco, USA/Wikimedia Commons, CC BY 2.0
Man blowing shofar	© Kobby Dagan/Shutterstock
Jews painting their door lintels with lamb's blood	Wikimedia Commons
Matzo bread	© picturepartners/Shutterstock
Girls dancing	Z. Radovan/www.BibleLandPictures.com
Jewish trumpets	© david156/Shutterstock
Sukkah	© ChameleonsEye/Shutterstock
Hannukah	© Noam Armonn/Shutterstock
Purim celebration	Z. Radovan/www.BibleLandPictures.com

Where Is the Newborn?

Caesar Augustus	© 2012 by Zondervan
Modern-day Bethlehem	© Przemyslaw Skibinski/Shutterstock
Nativity scene	© PixelDarkroom/Shutterstock
Dove mosaic	ToddBolen/www.BiblePlaces.com, taken at the Domus Romana Museum
Planisphere	Wikimedia Commons
Map of Joseph and Mary's travels	Map by International Mapping. Copyright © by Zondervan.
Joseph and family travel to Egypt	Public Domain

Fishermen, Followers, and Friends

Fisherman tossing net	© Ryan Rodrick Beiler/Shutterstock
Map to the Galilee boat	Map by International Mapping. Copyright © by Zondervan.
Galilee boat	Wikimedia Commons
Money changer	© Baker Publishing Group and Dr. James C. Martin. Courtesy of the Eretz Israel Museum, Tel Aviv, Israel.
Pilate coin	Wikimedia Commons
Capernaum synagogue ruins	© Noam Armonn/Shutterstock
Ancient sandals	Z. Radovan/www.BibleLandPictures.com

Could He Be the One?

Map of Jesus' ministry	Map by International Mapping. Copyright © by Zondervan.
Baptism at the Jordan River	© Eunika Sopotnicka/Shutterstock
Judean wilderness	© 1995 by Phoenix Data Systems
Location of the Sermon on the Mount	© Sopotnicki/Shutterstock
Lord's prayer on the walls of the Pater Noster	© suronin/Shutterstock
Jacob's well	Ferrell Jenkins/www.BiblePlaces.com
Ceiling of Church of the Transfiguration	© Anastazzo/Shutterstock
Sheepfold	© 1993 by Zondervan

Teaching with Parables

Parable of the sower	Wikimedia Commons
Wheat	© Ricardo Reitmeyer/Shutterstock
Mustard seeds	Gordon Franz
Grapevine	Todd Bolen/www.BiblePlaces.com
Ancient inn	Library of Congress, LC-DIG-ppmsca-02718/www.LifeintheHolyLand.com
Parable of the lost coin	Providence Collection/GoodSalt
Carob pods	© Claudio Rampinini/Shutterstock
Israeli wedding feast	© 1993 by Zondervan

Crowded Streets and Angry Mobs

Map of Galilee	Map by International Mapping. Copyright © by Zondervan.
John fragment	Centre for Public Christianity
Rembrandt's painting Christ in the Storm on the Lake of Galilee	Wikimedia Commons
Pools of Bethesda	Wikimedia Commons/Ariely, CC BY 3.0
Fish and bread	Wikimedia Commons
Tilapia	© nednapa/Shutterstock
Tomb of Lazarus	Todd Bolen/www.BiblePlaces.com

Enter the Gates of the Holy City

Western wall of temple area	© mikhail/Shutterstock

"He Wept Over it"
by Enrique Simonet — Wikimedia Commons
Model of Jerusalem — Wikimedia Commons
Herod's palace — © 1995 by Phoenix Data Systems
Herod family tomb — Paul Arps/Wikimedia Commons, CC BY 2.0
Palm Sunday — © Ryan Rodrick Beiler/Shutterstock
Antonia Fortress — © William D. Mounce

▶ The Dark Day

Map of Jerusalem during
Jesus' final days — Map by International Mapping. Copyright © by Zondervan.
Communion — © IngridHS/Shutterstock
Garden of Gethsemane — © kavram/Shutterstock
30 pieces of silver — Z. Radovan/www.BibleLandPictures.com
Roman scourge — © 1993 by Zondervan
Jesus nailed to the cross — © welburnstuart/Shutterstock
Garden Tomb — © 2015 by Zondervan

▶ Lies, Rumors, and Hope

Tomb with rolling stone — © William D. Mounce
Myrrh — © FooTToo/Shutterstock
Women at the empty tomb — © Nancy Bauer/Shutterstock
Road to Emmaus — Wikimedia Commons
Mount of Olives — © Renata Sedmakova/Shutterstock
Jerusalem East Gate — © William D. Mounce

▶ The Messiah

Tree of Jesse — Ms 21926 The Tree of Jesse from a psalter, English School/British Library, London, UK/Bridgeman Images
Mother and child — © Zurijeta/Shutterstock
Manger — © William D. Mounce
Nazareth — AP Images/Dan Balilty
Capernaum — © vblinov/Shutterstock
Jesus driving out money
changers from the temple — William Brassey Hole/Private Collection/© Look and Learn/Bridgeman Images
Donkey foal — © sarra22/Shutterstock

▶ How Did the Church Get Started?

Map of Pentecost — Map by International Mapping. Copyright © by Zondervan.
Upper room — © Peter Zaharov/Shutterstock
Woodcut of Pentecost — Planet Art
Location of stoning of Stephen — © Aleksandar Todorovic/Shutterstock
House in Joppa — © OPIS Zagreb/Shutterstock
The Sanhedrin — © Faithlife Corporation, makers of Logos Bible Software–www.logos.com
2nd Peter fragment — Wikimedia Commons
Nero coin — Clinton E. Arnold

▶ When Rome Ruled the World

Roman catapult replica — © Yory Frenklakh/Shutterstock
Hippodrome recreation of ruins — © William D. Mounce
Roman charioteer — © 2013 by Zondervan
Caesarea Maritima — Balage Balogh/www.archaeologyillustrated.com
Coastal home at Caesarea
Maritima — © ChameleonsEye/Shutterstock
Roman war ship — © Linda Bucklin/Shutterstock
Breach in wall at Gamla — Todd Bolen/www.BiblePlaces.com
Boulders in Jerusalem — www.HolyLandPhotos.org
Arch of Titus — © Matt Ragen/Shutterstock

▶ Those in Charge

Josephus — Wikimedia Commons
The Pharisees Question Jesus — illustration for 'The Life of Christ', c.1886-96, Tissot, James Jacques Joseph/Brooklyn Museum of Art, New York, USA/Bridgeman Images
Ossuary of Caiphus — Wikimedia Commons

Huldah gate — © 1995 by Phoenix Data Systems
Mikveh — Todd Bolen/www.BiblePlaces.com
Priests' court temple recreation — A. D. Riddle/www.BiblePlaces.com
Western wall — © Elisei Shafer/www.123RF.com
Dome of the Rock — © 2015 by Zondervan

▶ Strange Idols and Prison Cells

Paul cave painting — © Baker Publishing Group and Dr. James C. Martin
Roman citizenship bronze — Kim Walton. The British Museum.
Straight Street in Damascus — © 1995 by Phoenix Data Systems
Antioch — Todd Bolen/www.BiblePlaces.com
Philippi jail — © 1995 by Phoenix Data Systems
Artemis statue — © mountainpix/Shutterstock
Corinthian judgement seat — © 1995 by Phoenix Data Systems

▶ Shipwrecks and Caesar

Guards protect Paul — GoodSalt/Pacific Press
Herod's palace at Caesarea — © Sopotnicki/Shutterstock
Ancient Roman cargo ship — Z. Radovan/www.BibleLandPictures.com
Appian Way — © Francisco Javier Diaz/Shutterstock
Map of Rome in NT times — Copyright © 2011 by Zondervan
Bust of Emperor Nero — Gordon Franz
Mamertine Prison — Todd Bolen/www.BiblePlaces.com

▶ Writing the Rest of the Bible

Patmos — © Marlaine/Bigstock
Jesus as the conquering king — © Anilah/Shutterstock
Romans reading scrolls — Relief depicting a school scene, from Neumagen, Gallo-Roman/Rheinisches Landesmuseum, Trier, Germany/Bridgeman Images
Modern-day Jew reading scroll — © Aleksandar Todorovic/Shutterstock
Codex Sinaiticus — Z. Radovan/www.BibleLandPictures.com
New Testament scribe — Landsdowne 1179 f.34v Scribe at his desk comparing two books, from Le Miroir Historiale, c.1340, French School/British Library, London, UK/© British Library Board. All Rights Reserved/Bridgeman Images
John Wycliffe — Wikimedia Commons
Wycliffe Bible — Page from Wycliffe's translation of the Bible into English c1400. The bygynynge of ye gospel of Jesus Christ ye sone of God St Mark's gospel. John Wycliffe. English religious reformer. After Egerton manuscript./Universal History Archive/UIG   Bridgeman Images
King James Bible — Public Domain

▶ Who's Who in the Old Testament

Statue of David — © alefbet/Shutterstock
Painting of Moses — Wikimedia Commons
Statue of Michael the archangel — © Buturlimov Paul/Shutterstock

▶ Who's Who in the New Testament

Coin of Caesar Augustus — Jay King
Mosaic portrait of Paul — Wikimedia Commons
Simeon — Wikimedia Commons